LOOKING FOR HEROES

One Boy, One Year, 100 Letters

AIDAN COLVIN

WITH LIISA OGBURN

ISBN-13:978-1540788030

Second Edition, design and typeset by Brian Johnson

Printed in the United States of America

A hero is someone who, in spite of weakness, doubt or not always knowing the answers, goes ahead and overcomes anyway.
— Christopher Reeve

TABLE OF CONTENTS

Acknowledgments   vii

1 The Idea   2

2 Getting Started   10

3 Blending In   18

4 What Are Your Strengths?   24

5 Waiting   32

6 The First Letter   38

7 Dreams   44

8 Fake It Til You Make It   50

9 Arming Oneself   60

10 Looking For One Thing, Finding Another   66

11 Improvise   72

12 Try   80

13 Things Take The Time They Take   86

14 A New School   94

15 Jack   100

16 Storms   104

17 The First Interview   110

18 The First Regatta   118

19 Pop   124

20 The Ninth Letter   130

21 Endings   136

22 The Jay Leno Show   140

23 Welcome To The Real World   146

ACKNOWLEDGMENTS

First and foremost, we want to thank the dyslexics who responded to Aidan's letters, including Dr. Delos Cosgrove, Diane Swonk, John Irving, Thomas Sayre, Ben Foss, Harvey Hubbel, Phillip Schultz, Princess Beatrice, Ann Bancroft and Jay Leno. Without their wisdom and generosity, this project simply wouldn't exist. Furthermore, we may have let these letters gather dust in a desk drawer had it not been for the early enthusiasm and encouragement from our agent Kerry Sparks at Levine Greenberg Rostan Literary Agency and Executive Editor David Linker of Harper Collins. Tricia Wilson, Helen Crouse, Jenny Doyle, Erin Duffy and Alice O'Hair provided invaluable feedback and editing along the way. Kate O'Brien connected us with Fayetteville Observer writer Bill Kirby, who brought Aidan backstage to meet Jay Leno when he performed in Fayetteville, NC. Kate also called us on a weekly basis to cheer us on through the final production tasks. Rodney Hartman mentored us through the process of publishing on Amazon. Finally, the real heroes in Aidan's story and in the stories of kids like him are the parents and teachers who encourage and help kids with learning differences succeed. We simply cannot thank you enough.

March 15, 2016

Dear Mr. Leno,

I've written you three times now.

I know you're busy. In fact I know a lot about you. I know you won your first prize for comedy while you were a french fry cutter at McDonald's. I know you did standup at strip clubs during college. I know you wrote for TV. I know you're one of the most successful comedians ever. Ever.

I also know you're dyslexic.

That's why I'm writing. I want a map from here where I sit, as a dyslexic tenth grader floundering in chemistry and algebra, to there where you are, "making it."

What's the key? One dyslexic to another?

Over the last year, I've written 100 letters to dyslexics. I've heard back from people like Writer John Irving, Arctic Explorer Ann Bancroft, Cleveland Clinic President Dr. Delos Cosgrove... But I really want to hear back from you.

There are not a lot of successful people out there who started out in special ed and ended up a success. But you did. How? What made the difference? Will you answer just a few questions? I can ask you in person—if you'd prefer. I see you're performing in Fayetteville, NC next month. Do you have 10 minutes for an interview? If so, I'll be there. I'm serious. If that can't work, I'd still be thrilled to get your answers by phone or Skype or mail or email.

I'm enclosing my book. Your response would make a spectacular ending. That said, I've learned a lot just through writing it. Well, thanks.

Yours sincerely,

1 THE IDEA

Alright, you're probably wondering how this whole thing got started. I mean, how did a kid like me—nervous, short, braces, learning disability—start on a project like this?

A midnight bolt of inspiration?

Not exactly. That might be a good formula for an afterschool special, but it wouldn't be the truth. And that's what I want to tell you: the truth.

It was the summer before tenth grade. You know, the grade—according to your guidance counselor—that counts. And school wasn't my strong suit. Honestly, I was at a loss for what my strong suit was. While most of my friends were taking robotics and AP this or Honors that, I was staying after school for math tutoring. I was spending lunch with the chemistry teacher (and not because I had a crush on her). I was spending Friday nights watching YouTube history videos. While my friends were studying for the SAT and beginning to visit colleges, I was seriously considering the "Help Wanted" sign at Snoopy's Hotdogs and Grill.

I seemed to be failing at this thing called life before it had even started.

Why? I have something called dyslexia. You know what that is? Most think it's this cute little thing that makes you switch your b's and d's or write things backwards. And I did do that. I still do.

But it's more than that. It's a difference in how my brain sees writing and then attaches sounds to letters.

The best I can explain is to point you to this picture that Daniel Britton, a designer in London, made to show what dyslexics see

D Ͻ
G ͻ
J ǀ
M Ʌ
P Ͻ
S ͼ
V ⁄

when they look at the alphabet. The letters on the left show what you probably see. The letters on the right show what people like me see. Dan got it right.

If you're like me, reading or having to handwrite something is like running a race as a double amputee. It takes every damn cell in your brain. And I still come in last. That's one consistency: In school, I almost always come in last.

Don't get me wrong. Dyslexia is not a life-or-death kind of big deal. My granddad "Pop," who lives with us, he's got cancer. I'm not walking around with a cane or struggling to eat or breathe. I know what that looks like. But maybe that's what makes this a little more challenging? It's invisible. Well, until you have to write something. Or read aloud. Or take one of those damn standardized tests. Or...

Cry me a river, Dad would say.

I know. It's one long, sorry list of what I can't do.

What *can* I do?

Good question.

The idea for this project all started the first day of summer. I had just finished ninth grade at Research Triangle High School. My mom and I were cleaning out my room. Whenever she feels like things are kind of out of control, she focuses all her anxiety on cleaning. Some moms go to Zumba. Mine pulls out the vacuum cleaner.

"Fresh start," she said. It was a statement rather than a question.

She had made three gargantuan piles of crap in the hallway: Keep, Donate, Trash.

I like to be around when she's making these decisions. Her tendency is to put everything of mine in the Trash pile.

"Donate?" She held up a favorite soccer jersey that was way too small.

"No!" I said.

She tossed it in the "Donate" pile anyway. She pointed to the Darth Vader coin bank.

"Keep," I said, firmly.

She looked at it for a minute, conceded and put it in a box to go to the attic.

She then held up a poster we had made together in fifth grade called "Dyslexic Heroes."

"Definitely keep," I said.

We had made it the year I returned to public school. See, I went to a private school for kids with "learning disabilities" for second, third and fourth grade. On the first day back to public school in fifth grade, I heard a girl ask her friend, "Is he new?" pointing at me. Her friend had said, "Nah. He went here, but then went off to some special school."

People say things like that enough and you start to believe them.

"Not true," Mom had said when I told her.

"Right." I had rolled my eyes.

"I'll show you." She had opened her computer and googled "famous dyslexics."

And you know who popped up?

Jay Leno. Yeah. Jay Leno! Whoopi Goldberg. Steven Spielberg... Harrison Ford. Albert Einstein. Walt Disney. What the heck?

"Those girls just don't know what dyslexia is," Mom had said.

So when my fifth grade teacher told us to research something, I had chosen dyslexia. I made the poster my mom was holding up right now.

She looked at me.

"I want to keep that," I said, "up."

"Okay," she said and tacked it up over my desk.

"Nervous about going to a new school?" she asked.

DYSLEXICS

SLOW READERS, OUT-OF-THE-BOX THINKERS

Once we accept our limits, we go beyond them. -Albert Einstein

If I had not been dyslexic, I would not have won the Olympic decathlon games. Dyslexia made me outwork the next guy. -Bruce Jenner

I get stubborn and dig in when people tell me I can't do something and I think I can. - Ann Bancroft

If you can dream it, you can do it. - Walt Disney

Don't let what you can't do in life stop you from what you can do. - John Wooden

I truly feel that my difficulty in reading and spelling is a small price to pay for these natural gifts in other areas. - Beryl Benacerraf

Life is full of challenges. How you handle them is what builds character. -Erin Brockovich

I believe that the reason I've been able to discover the things my very intelligent colleagues couldn't is because of my dyslexia. I look at things from a different perspective. - Dr. R. Wyatt

VISIT: HTTP://WWW.DYSLEXIC-KIDS.COM/
FOR MORE POSITIVE MESSAGES FOR KIDS

SCOTT ADAMS
MUHAMMED ALI
LUDWIG VAN BEETHOVEN
RICHARD BRANSON
ERIN BROCKOVICH
GEORGE BURNS
GEORGE BUSH
GEORGE HW BUSH
STEVEN CANNEL
JOHN T. CHAMBERS
JACKIE CHAN
CHER
AGATHA CHRISTIE
WINSTON CHURCHILL
TOM CRUISE
LEONARDO DA VINCI
PATRICK DEMPSEY
WALT DISNEY
THOMAS EDISON
EIFFEL
ALBERT EINSTEIN
HENRY FONDA
HARRISON FORD
BENJAMIN FRANKLIN
BILL GATES
WHOOPIE GOLDBERG
ALEXANDER GRAHAM BELL
WOODY HARRELSON
SALMA HAYEK
WILLIAM HEWLETT
STONEWALL JACKSON
THOMAS JEFFERSON
BRUCE JENNER
JEWEL
STEVE JOBS
MAGIC JOHNSON
JOHN F. KENNEDY
KEIRA KNIGHTLY
JOHN LENNON
JAY LENO
PAUL ORFALEA
OZZY OZBOURNE
GEORGE PATTON
PABLO PICASO
KEENU REEVES
BABE RUTH
CHARLES SCHWAB
SUZANNE SOMMERS
STEVEN SPIELBRG
JACKIE STEWART
TED TURNER
LIV TYLER
GEORGE WASHINGTON
OPRAH WINFREY
ROBIN WILLIAMS
WOODROW WILSON
F.W. WOOLWORTH

LOOKING FOR HEROES

I was transferring from a small public charter an hour away to a small public high school close-by.

I looked down.

"You're going to be fine," she said.

I grunted. She stopped cleaning.

"It is going to be hard," she started. "But you've learned how to..."

"Not fail?" I interrupted her.

"...succeed," she said.

"Really?" I was dubious.

"You're resourceful," she said.

"I'm tired," I said.

She paused and looked at the poster. "I wonder how those guys made it..."

We both looked at it.

"Smarter," I mumbled.

She shook her head. "You could ask."

"Right," I said, sarcastically.

"Yeah, write!" she said.

"What?"

"Write them a letter!" she said.

"A dyslexic write a dyslexic?" I asked.

She shrugged.

"No one would write back," I said.

"What if they did?" she countered.

We both went silent.

I looked at my desk. It was clean. I have to admit, I like it when my mom goes OCD on my room. Pencils, erasers, paper clips, highlighters, each in their own container.

She picked up a box for Goodwill and pointed at another box, "Attic."

I nodded.

Then she started humming that song by Sting.

"I hope that someone gets my.... I hope that someone gets my...."

I listened to her feet clomping down the stairs. "...message in a bottle," she continued singing.

I looked at the poster again. I remembered Mom and me combing through the web looking for pictures and quotes. I remembered coming across Ann Bancroft, the first woman to reach the North and South Poles and to cross Antarctica. When someone asked her how she did it, she said, "I get stubborn and dig in when people tell me I can't do something and I think I can."

I opened up my laptop and googled Ann now.

A photo came up. She was wearing a neon orange ski jacket and standing next to a dog sled. Icicles hung from her hair. She looked electric.

How did she get from point A to point B? From special ed to the South Pole?

I saw a link to a recent interview she did. I clicked on it.

I honed in on something she said about a book called *Endurance*. It's about Ernest Shackleton's failed expedition to Antarctica.

"The ship was frozen, but what came off the pages was adventure, camaraderie, and being out in the hinterland where no one had ever been before. I wanted to make history when I was a kid because of that book."

I wanted to make history, too.

But how does someone like me... do something extraordinary, like that?

What was Ann's secret?

And that's how this crazy, terrifying, impossible, pea-brained project started. I decided I was going to write Ann. I was going to ask her. And I wasn't going to stop with her. I was going to write 100 successful dyslexics.

I was going to ask each of them if they had one piece of advice—just one—for a kid like me. Since they had once been a kid like me.

It was likely no one would write back.

Then I remembered a story about Thomas Edison.

He was supposedly dyslexic.

And when he was seven, his teacher told his mom he was too "dull" for school. So his mom pulled him out.

His mom told him his teacher was wrong. She home-schooled him.

By ten, he was doing experiments in the back shed. Years later, while he was working on his most famous invention, a reporter asked Edison how he felt after one more experiment failed.

You know what he said? He said, "I've not failed. I've just found 10,000 ways that won't work."

At the time, he was working on the light bulb.

We all know how that story ends.

And this is how my story begins.

2 GETTING STARTED

Let's get this straight. I'm dyslexic, right? My writing stinks. I think in pictures. When I can, I use pictures. Especially when my words get all jumbled up and fall into a heap. Or when pictures say it better than words. Like this one. It's a picture of my family. I need to introduce them to you because they're a big part of my story.

It's a picture from last Christmas. There's my granddad, "Pop" (striped monkey suit, far right). He's the one who gave our whole family onesies last Christmas. There's Aunt Hillary to the left of him (we call her "ant hill"). She's the one who gave us blue wigs so we could play blue-haired bingo on Christmas Eve. My dad is in the spotted cow pajamas with the rock star wig. To the left of dad is his sister Sherri and her husband Gary.

My mom has the tall Marge Simpson wig. I'm wearing the superman onesy up front on left. Livia, my younger sister, is the unicorn, front and center. And Sarah, who is younger than Liv and right behind her, is in pig pj's. Fitting. Believe me.

What does this picture have to do with this story? You should know up front my family's a little odd. And the apple doesn't fall far from the tree.

Anyway, it was the second day of summer. I had slept in. I could hear lawnmowers in the Coleman's yard. I stood up, stretched and sat down at my clean desk. I looked out the window.

I could hear my two sisters downstairs. Liv is twelve and Sarah's almost ten. They were packing a picnic. Our neighbors, Anna and Joey, were over helping. They were getting ready to bike down to the Oakwood Cemetery.

It's close. You just turn left out our front door, then left on Polk. Go four blocks. Polk t-bones into Linden. And there's a gate there that's kind of hidden behind the shrubbery. You have to know about it to see it. But once you see it, you can't un-see it. It's held closed with a loose neon yellow rope. When you lift the rope, the gate swings inward and after you carry your bike down the steps and refasten the gate, you're set. Miles of paths. The occasional car during funeral hours, but mostly nobody. We once saw a pack of three deer back there and a fox and its kits, too.

Hard to believe because we live in downtown Raleigh. Raleigh, North Carolina. We live on Person Street. It's this four-lane through-way. In the mornings, everyone drives in from the suburbs. In the evenings, everyone drives out. They fly by honking and yelling. Not exactly conducive for deer. Or fox. Rats? Yes. (They're about the size of our dogs). Raccoon, possum? Yes and yes. Deer? No.

"Breakfast?" Mom stuck her head in my door.

"Not hungry," I said.

"What are you doing?" she asked.

"I'm going to start writing those letters," I said.

"Aidan!" Pop yelled from downstairs. "Aidan!"

"Yep?" I yelled down.

"I need help."

I looked at my mom.

"I'm going to find ten names and addresses today," I said matter-of-factly.

She smiled.

"Aidan!" Pop called up again.

"Coming," I said. I stood up and walked past her. I went downstairs. Pop was in the den on the couch. "Pop," my dad's dad, moved in with us last year when he was diagnosed with advanced cancer. He was often up, shaved and showered when I came down for breakfast.

"I can't figure this darn thing out," he said. He was holding an iPhone Uncle Bryan had given him.

"I'll show you." I plopped down next to him.

Pop's dyslexic, too.

"I need to text Sherri," he said. Sherri is his daughter.

I pushed the button on the front and said slowly, "Text Sherri."

Siri opened the texting app and said, "What do you want to say to Sherri?"

I motioned for Pop to say something.

Pop said, "This is Pop" and watched as the application typed in his message. He added, "My grandson is so smart." It typed that, too.

"Done?" I whispered.

"Yep," he said back.

"Press this," I said, pointing to the "send" button.

His fingers were big and swollen. See, Pop spent forty-two years cutting hair in the Cape Fear Hotel

Barbershop he ran on Second Street near the waterfront in Wilmington.

He pressed it.

"Thanks, my grandson!" he said, smiling.

"Is that all?" I asked.

"How about a sticky bun down at Yellow Dog?" he asked.

"Got to do something first," I said.

AIDAN'S TIP

If you're dyslexic and haven't discovered dictation yet, your life is about to change. No joke. I dictate my homework, long answers on tests, emails, texts... If I had a girlfriend, I'd dictate my love letters. Maybe Jay Leno can help me with that?

"You know where to find me," he said.

I nodded. I looked out the back door. It was gorgeous out. What was I doing? Right. I was going to write.

I walked back up to my room. I could hear a cement truck backing up to the construction site across the street. New condos were going up. The truck was making that annoying beeping sound. Beep, beep, beep, beeeeep.

I couldn't concentrate. Maybe I should go downstairs and get a coke? Something to wake up my brain?

Beep, beep, beep, beeeeep.

I was going to pull out all my hair if that darn...

I looked around for earplugs. I couldn't find any so I slipped on my headphones.

Now, who to write? I thought. I googled "famous dyslexics."

Jay Leno, Whoopi Goldberg, Harrison Ford, Keira Knightly. Keira Knightly?

I looked at her picture. Man, she was hot. I'd seen her somewhere. Oh, yeah. Pirates of the Caribbean.

She was dyslexic? How could a dyslexic become an actress? How do they read all those lines? I'd ask her! I copied and pasted her name, right after Ann Bancroft. I added names of other actors and actresses, and a surgeon whose name kept coming up. Dr. Cosgrove. Until I had seven, eight, nine. Ten. Done.

Ann Bancroft, Polar Explorer
Keira Knightley, Actress
Whoopi Goldberg, Actress and Comedian
Jay Leno, Comedian
Harrison Ford, Actor
Henry Winkler, Actor and Writer
Dr. Toby Cosgrove, Surgeon
Jennifer Aniston, Actress
Billy Bob Thornton, Actor
Johnny Depp, Actor

I stretched. That wasn't so hard. Now addresses...

I found Ann Bancroft and Dr. Cosgrove pretty quick. But the movie stars? Everyone had these "Fan Mail" addresses. They said "Send a SASE." What's that? I googled it. "Self-addressed stamped envelope." Why? I scrolled down. Oh, for an autographed picture.

I didn't want an autographed picture.

I wanted answers. I wanted to know how these folks got from special ed to the top of the universe?

My mom came to stand in my doorway. "Want a ride to Levi's?"

"In a minute," I said, distractedly, scrolling through the results.

"I'll be in my office," she said. She stepped out.

I've known Levi since sixth grade. I love seeing him cause he still likes to do dumb stuff like have nerf gun wars or food dares. Maybe I should just put this aside until tomorrow? I stared out the window for minute.

Yeah. Yeah. Good idea. I stood up. No. No. No. Bad idea. I sat back down.

If I put it off today, I'd come up with another excuse tomorrow. I bet Thomas Edison didn't use a lot of excuses.

I let out a long breath. I started searching for addresses again. Fan mail, fan mail, fan mail. Nothing else. Nada. I got back up and went to my mom's office. She was hunched over her laptop. Her back was to me. I tapped on the glass. I waited a second to see if she heard me. She didn't. I tapped on the door again. She still didn't hear me. I opened the door.

"What?" she whipped around in her chair.

She pulled two spongy purple earplugs out and took a deep breath, trying not to yell. She placed them down on the desk. My dad had made the desk for her out of some planks he found dumpster diving. He had sanded it to a smooth finish.

"Can you help me?" I asked. "I can't find addresses." She stood up and we walked to my room. I carried her chair so we could sit at my desk together.

She looked at my list. I had Jay Leno's contact info up on the screen.

She magnified the screen. "Hmmm," she said.

"Just for autographs," I said.

"Found any others?" she asked.

"Dr. Cosgrove and Ann Bancroft..." I said, half-heartedly.

She googled Jay Leno again, then scrolled through the pages of results. She found the same address I did.

"I don't know how to get in touch with movie stars," she admitted. "Just send it to fan mail."

"But look," I said. I scrolled to the comments below the address. "Everyone says they didn't get a response."

"If it were easy...." She stood up and picked up her chair.

"Fine," I said, annoyed.

I let out a long breath.

Her eyebrows twitched. I knew she wanted to say something but was holding her tongue.

"Probably a waste of time," I said.

"Maybe," she said. She carried her chair back to her office. She called over her shoulder, "maybe not..."

I sat back down. Slowly, one by one, I found addresses for ten. Most were fan mail addresses. That was the best I could do. I wanted to hear from people like Harrison Ford and Jay Leno. Especially Jay Leno. I wasn't ready to take those names off the list.

Done. I saved the document and printed it. I looked at it. I stood up and stretched. I started pacing.

Were these guys really dyslexic?

And if they were, what was their secret?

I mean, How did Jay Leno become Jay Leno?

If I could figure that out...

But I was jumping ahead of myself.

It was more likely that no one would write back.

I let out a long breath. I put the list down and headed for the kitchen.

Whatever happened, I did know one thing: I wasn't going to figure out how any of these folks became who they are while sitting around waiting for them to tell me.

I had to ask them.

I had to find a way to ask them.

And that was what I was going to do.

3 BLENDING IN

I don't know about you, but I like to fly under the radar.

When I was in the first and second grade, when the teacher would call on me to identify a letter or read a word or a sentence... well, it was like having my skin rubbed down with sandpaper. Excruciating. All eyes were on you.

I couldn't read a thing. I could barely write the five letters in my name. It wasn't for lack of trying. Almost every night in kindergarten, first and second grade, my mom would sit on the edge of my bed. She'd point to a word on a page in front of me. She'd sound out each letter.

"Cccc– Aaaa– Tttt. Cat."

"Rrrr– Aaaa– Ttt. Rat."

Into my head the sounds would go, roll around like dice, and then when I would try to read the word back, out something else would come.

I couldn't remember what letters had what sounds. I'd sit there. She'd wait. I'd guess. Almost always wrong. And then we'd start over.

What was wrong with me?

I begged, "Homeschool me."

"I can't," she said.

> **AIDAN'S TIPS**
>
> *Things to do if you're called on to read aloud in class or church or boy scouts or... (fill in the blank):*
>
> - *Stop, drop and roll.*
> - *Begin speaking French.*
> - *Knock your knees together, scrunch up your face and point to the bathroom.*
> - *Start to bark.*
> - *DO NOT CRY (even if that's what you want to do). Do NOT let them see you cry.*

Eventually, she and my dad met with my teachers.

"Everyone develops at different rates," one teacher said.

"Have you checked his eyes?" suggested another.

"Yes," Mom answered, then anticipating the next question, said, "and his hearing."

"Color blind?" another person asked, "colored overlays helped one kid I knew."

Mom ordered them. She ordered a million things. (Talking dictionaries, computer word games, a pen that reads print, flash cards, Bob books...)
Nothing helped.

One teacher said, "Not all kids are cut out for school."

I won't tell you what Mom said to that.

My school said they didn't test for learning disabilities until third grade. I told my parents I was going to drop out before then.

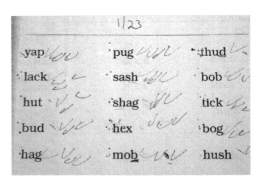

My parents decided to have me tested privately.

We went to 3Cs Family Services in the next town. The waiting room had beige-carpets with uncomfortable olive and squash-colored couches. My little sisters would toddle over to the cardboard blocks while I waited for my name to be called. I remember looking around the room at all the other kids

AIDAN'S MOM'S TIP

Dr. Sally Shaywitz, Director of Yale's Center for Dyslexia and Creativity, says you can and should test for dyslexia as early as kindergarten — especially if someone else in the family has it.

sitting quietly with their parents. It was a sad place. We were all broken somehow.

After three mornings of testing, Dr. Adams called me and my mom and dad back to his office.

He sat us down. He let out a long breath and then turned to me and said, "Aidan, this is totally fixable."

Really?

"You're dyslexic," he said.

"Dis-what?" I asked.

"It's a learning difference," he said. "Your brain just works a little differently."

AIDAN'S MOM'S TIP

Some states recognize dyslexia and you can get pretty good, free help in the public schools. NC does not which means that its special education teachers aren't trained in the instructional methods that are proven to work best. To make matters worse, at 46th in the nation for education spending, NC's special ed teachers must often work with many kids with very different learning needs all at once. Once Aidan was identified for special education and pulled out, we saw that not only was special ed not helping, he was falling more behind and his confidence was plunging. We moved him in second grade to a specialized private school for three years.

"Am I ever going to be able to read?" I asked.

"Yes," he said, "but you'll learn quicker if you work with someone who knows how to teach dyslexics." He paused, "there are special schools," then added, "you wouldn't need to go forever—just a few years."

I didn't want to leave my friends.

He turned to my parents. "Does someone else in your family have it? Eight out of ten dyslexics have a close family member with it."

Dad said, "Pop's got it."

I started working with a tutor almost immediately. Three times a week afterschool, my mom dropped me off at Ms. Lou Little's white house with four big columns. For an hour we would sit at her dining room table and go through lists of short words with different sounds over and over and over. And over.

I was still falling behind. So in second grade my parents moved me to a private school just for kids with learning disabilities.

It was far from home. I didn't know anyone. It was small. Everyone was slow. And it was a relief. It was such a relief.

That's where I met Ms. Honeycutt. She was slender with neatly pinned back chestnut hair. She had freckles. She was kind and smiled a lot, but that first morning she was serious. She told us that while we might not believe it, we were smart. She told us that we simply had a difference in how we saw things. She assured us that, with effort, each of us would learn to read. She said she could say this with absolute certainty—absolute certainty—because she herself was dyslexic.

It was the first time an adult had ever told me they had dyslexia.

AIDAN'S MOM'S TIP

Soon after Aidan moved to a private school with other kids with similar learning issues, his anxiety went down (and so did ours). As he learned to use tools (such as dictation, screen readers, spell checkers, online calculators, customizable practice tests and websites that complemented what he was learning in the classroom), his confidence and grades went up. While a real financial and logistical stretch to make it work, it changed his academic trajectory. He returned to a regular classroom in the public school system in fifth grade.

"It's just another thing that describes me, Aidan," Ms. Honeycutt had said matter-of-factly. "Just like I have brown hair and blue eyes."

One day Ms. Honeycutt read us a chapter from this funny story called *Hank Zipzer: The World's Greatest Underachiever*. See, the main character, Hank, was dyslexic and always getting into trouble. The guy who came up with Hank is also dyslexic. His name is Henry Winkler and he's an actor.

Ms. Honeycutt told us that Henry Winkler was coming to Quail Ridge Books the following week and that we could meet him in person. So my mom and I went.

Quail Ridge was packed. Henry was funny and used his hands a lot while speaking. You could tell he was an actor. After he read the first chapter, he offered to sign books. The line wound around from the front of the store to the back. It moved slowly. He took the time to talk to each person.

When I finally got up to the table, I told him my name and that I was dyslexic, too. He suddenly got really, really serious.

He looked me right in the eye and you know what he said? He said, "Aidan, we've all got strengths. What are yours?"

I didn't know what to say.

Then he said, "Whatever they are, you run with them!"

I bought the first three books in his series. He signed them.

"You are great. — Henry Winkler"

I didn't know if I agreed with him, but somehow coming from him... Well, it was like when Ms. Honeycutt promised I would learn to read. It meant something.

• • •

I leaned back in my chair now and fiddled with the knobs on my desk drawer. I looked at my computer.

Find my strengths. How does one go about doing that? I didn't know.

I googled famous dyslexics again.

There were a lot. A lot more than I thought. I added more names to my list:

Ozzie Osbourne, Musician
John Irving, Writer
Phillip Schultz, Poet
Steven Spielberg, Filmmaker
Tommy Hilfiger, Clothes Designer
David Boies, Lawyer
Tim Tebow, Football Quarterback
Bruce Springsteen, Musician
Dav Pilkey, Writer
George Bush, Former President
Princess Beatrice, Granddaughter of Queen Elizabeth
Ted Turner, Businessman, Entrepreneur
Richard Branson, Entrepreneur

I wondered how each of these people had found their strengths.

I wondered how I was going to find mine.

What are your strengths?
Whatever they are, run with them.
— Henry Winkler

4 WHAT ARE YOUR STRENGTHS?

Strengths. Right. Strengths? Let's start with weaknesses.
I am:

Not athletic (usually picked last for teams)

Anxiety-prone

Not that great of a student (I try!)

Braces

Short. Very short. Very, very short.

This is where a picture speaks louder than words.

Yep, that's me and my friend Max. Same age. Exactly. Fifteen. No, Max is not a giant. I am a midget. Well, compared to just about every other boy in the tenth grade in the world.

All my friends' voices have changed. They shave. They've got hairy legs, enormous feet. My feet are pretty big. But with my luck that's the only thing that will be.

Dr. Burleson keeps saying, "One of these days... Aidan."

Blah, blah, blah...

Yeah, right, I want to say. Yawn.

My friend Cole made me this t-shirt for my last birthday: "Keep Calm and Stay Short."

"Oh, yeah," I told her, "No problem there."

The real problem is that Henry Winkler said, "Find your strengths."

How do you do that?

I started by asking my little sister Sarah.

"Sarah," I mumbled, "can you, um, help me on something?"

"Sure." She was in the den drawing on her white board. "What?" she said, without looking up.

"What are my strengths?"

She paused. "Well... you don't have a six pack...." She jumped up and lifted her pink, fluffy unicorn t-shirt to display her abs, "like me. Oh, yeah!"

"Do, too," I said. I lifted my shirt.

"Do not," Liv said, coming into the room.

I pleaded, "It's for a project."

I channeled Derrick from Zoolander and put my hands below my face and blinked my eyes. "It's really hard to be really, really, really ridiculously good-looking..."

"How would you know?" Liv replied coolly.

I scowled.

"Girls!" Mom said, entering the kitchen. Then, to me, "You're a people person, Aidan."

"Moms can't answer," I said.

Sarah said, going out the door, "I'm going to the Forno's."

"Me, too." Liv followed her out.

I followed them into the front hall. "Mom, don't you think they're getting sassy?"

She ignored my comment. She added, "You're also a hard worker."

I watched the girls disappear out the front door. Then I dictated "people person" and "hard worker" into the Notes App on my phone.

I wonder how Henry Winkler's family would have described him? They'd probably say something like, "We always knew Henry'd be a star because he was..."

"You're..." my mom interrupted me, then paused. "... kind," she said.

Kind? That's not the kind of word one uses to describe extraordinary people. It's what you say when you can't think of anything else to say. What about "courageous?"

Or "funny?" Or "good-looking?" "Kind?" Really?

I dictated "kind" into my phone anyway and padded upstairs in my socks.

I sat back down at my desk. Maybe I needed to forget about finding my strengths at this point and just write to people.

I opened up Word and decided to write arctic explorer Ann Bancroft first.

"Hi Ann,"

Nah. Too casual.

"Dear Ms. Bancroft,"

Too form letter.

"Dear Ms. Bancroft, How are you?"

Boring. I must have started a dozen times.

I knew Ms. Bancroft and everyone else I would write was super busy and couldn't tell me their whole story so I came up with four questions:

Who was your hero as a kid and why?

Can you point to someone or something that helped you become the success that you are?

Do you have a story from your life that might help me or others stay hopeful and keep trying when we've had a challenging setback?

What one piece of advice or wisdom would you give to a kid with dyslexia today?

Then I wrote and printed out twenty letters to the twenty dyslexics I'd identified so far. I signed them and printed out twenty sets of questions, too.

My sisters came back from the Forno's. Mom took Liv to gymnastics.

I asked Sarah if she could help stuff envelopes.

"Sure," she said. We set up an assembly line on the dining room table. Sarah helped address, seal and stamp each envelope. I included a self-addressed, stamped envelope so people could just pop their answers in the

Dear Ms. Bancroft,

I'm writing you because I'm looking for heroes.

My name is Aidan. I live in Raleigh, North Carolina with my parents, two younger sisters, two chubby dachshunds named Annie and Max and a hermit crab named Crabby. I love to run. I love to make movies I love to search for fossils with my dad and play practical jokes on my sisters. I also love to listen to stories, though I often struggle if I have to read them myself.

I'm writing you because I was born with a learning disability that makes reading really, really hard. I heard that you have dyslexia, too.

There aren't many successful people out there who started out in the special ed. classroom.

But you're one. Whenever I feel overwhelmed or discouraged, my mom points to people like you.

"How'd she do it?" I wondered aloud.

"Why not ask her?" my mom said.

That's why I'm writing.

How'd you do it? What made the difference? Will you tell me your story? I've enclosed some questions on the next sheet.

Sincerely,

mail to me when they were done.

Of course, I told them if they couldn't write (I mean, they're dyslexic), they could dictate their answers and email me. Or we could skype. Or I could come interview them in person. Or... the bottom line was I was flexible. When Sarah and I finished, I had a hefty pack of twenty letters. I felt the weight. She put a stamp on the last one and added it to the stack.

"Done," she said.

It looked good.

It felt good.

I did it.

And I did it not for school. Not for boy scouts. Not for church. I did it for me.

I carefully slid the stack into my backpack and hoisted it onto my back. I went out to the shed and wheeled my bike out. I opened the gate to the backyard, rolled the bike out onto the driveway and closed the gate behind me. I climbed on and headed south on Person Street.

I biked up to the four blue post boxes on New Bern Avenue. I checked the time of the last pickup. 5pm. It was 4:45. I had just made it.

I leaned my bike against the first box, pulled off the backpack and reached inside. I held the stack in my hands one last time.

What was I doing? I took a long, deep breath.

I said a prayer. Please let someone write back. Just one person. That's all I ask. Please?

Then I opened the squeaky blue door on the postbox and placed all the envelopes into the back. I let go. The door banged shut.

I opened the door again just to make sure all the envelopes had dropped down into the box. They had. Then I got back on my bike. I strapped on my helmet and turned my front tire towards home.

I had done it.

I had really done it. Something someone might even describe as "bold."

It got me thinking.

Ann Bancroft didn't just go out and one day become the first woman to cross the ice to the North Pole. She had to start somewhere. At my age she liked to camp in her backyard, even when it snowed. She had to teach herself how to set up a tent that didn't leak and how to stay warm in sub-zero weather. One thing led to another. Until, years later, she was invited to join an expedition to the North Pole. She became the first woman to reach the North Pole, and several years later, the South Pole, and then, after that, to cross Antarctica.

The stoplight on Person Street turned red. I braked and put my foot down.

What if someone did write me back?

The light turned green. I started pedaling again.

It might not lead me to the North Pole...

I started pedaling faster. The wind was rushing through my hair.

I remembered Thomas Edison's story. He didn't invent the light bulb after a single stroke of brilliance. He started doing experiments at seven. He was publishing a newspaper at 12. He got his first job at 15...

I skidded into my driveway. My heart was pounding.

I didn't need to know where this was going.

I couldn't know.

All I knew was the path I was on wasn't leading where I wanted to go. And maybe this one would.

5 WAITING

This morning, when I went down to get breakfast, Pop was sitting on the couch with his eyes closed. He opened them when he heard me.

"Good morning, my grandson!" he said.

"How are ya doing, Pop?" I asked.

"Not so well," my dad answered for him.

Dad had moved the floor lamp over to where Pop was sitting and was running his fingers along Pop's neck.

Pop bent his head to one side.

"Does that hurt?" Dad asked.

"No," he said. He noticed me standing there watching.

"What day is it today, Aidan?" Pop asked.

"Be still," Dad said.

"Tuesday?" I sat down on the couch and reached for the remote.

"Half-price hotdogs," we exclaimed and looked at each other at the same moment.

"Oww!" Pop said, pushing dad's hand off.

My dad let out a long breath. "I'm glad Dr. Spiritos could fit you in." He moved the floor lamp back to the corner.

There's this great hotdog joint not far from my house called Snoopy's. It's on the way to the hospital where Pop gets his treatment. It has this gigantic sign with a picture of a dancing hotdog. On Tuesdays, hotdogs cost just a buck. Two for $2.

Mom walked in with her car keys. "Ready, Pop?" she asked.

"Yep," he said. "Can we stop at Snoopy's?" He winked at me.

"Sure," she said.

Pop stood up and started to sway.

"Not so fast," Dad said, helping to steady him.

Pop had left his audiobook on in the next room. I could hear the narrator reading Master and Commander.

"You want me to turn it off?" I asked him.

He nodded, disoriented.

Mom handed him some ginger ale. "See if this helps."

He took a sip. His cell phone rang. He fumbled in his pocket to find it, saw who it was and turned it on speakerphone.

"Hello, my daughter!" his voice boomed out.

Why do all old people talk on speakerphone? We can hear all Pop's conversations. It's a good thing he doesn't talk about girlfriends or STDs or anything like that.

Dad's pager started going off. He pulled it off his belt, studied the number, turned it off and reached for his cell.

"Got to run," he said, dialing a number and walking out. "Call me if Spiritos has a minute to talk."

My dad used to write for a newspaper. He didn't decide to be a doctor until he was thirty. He was thirty-seven when he graduated. In fact, he was in school when I was born. Now he works as a doc at a hospital near our house.

I went into Pop's room and put the audiobook on pause. I straightened out the open suitcase he had on a table at the foot of the bed. I pulled the covers up and plumped up his pillow. Funny. Until recently, Pop hadn't read much. Now he listens to books all the time.

"It's a good thing I didn't know about audiobooks

earlier," he joked. "I never would have gotten anything done."

"I wouldn't have graduated from middle school," I told him.

When I have a lot to read for school, I even speed up the audio. At 1 ½ speed, it kind of sounds like Daffy Duck, but I've gotten used to it.

My mom tells me to read along with the print. "It builds word recognition," she says. Sometimes I do it. But it's tiring.

None of the dyslexics I've written so far had audiobooks growing up. Or Siri or dictation.

"How'd you graduate?" I asked Pop. He said he just took classes where he didn't have to read, or read much, like shop and woodworking.

And then, when he got married and had Aunt Sherri, he looked for a job that didn't require reading or good grades. He was very practical. Everyone needs haircuts, he thought, so he went to barber school. He opened his own barbershop. He supported his family on $3 and $5 and $7 haircuts and shaves, fourteen hours a day, five days a week for over forty years.

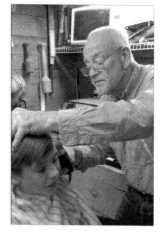

When he closed up shop, he moved one of his chairs to his garage. Customers still stop by for a trim or a shave or to shoot the breeze or share a coffee with Baileys Irish Creme.

That's where me and my dad and my sisters still get our haircuts.

"Mohawk?" he asked last time.

I shook my head. "Crew cut then," he said. He's always joking.

Pop never complained about what he couldn't do. He just got down and did what he could.

And you know what? He's pretty happy. Or he has been.

I looked over at him now sitting on the couch. He looked small and tired.

"Feel like you can stand up now?" Mom asked, looking at him carefully.

"Yep," Pop said and stood up more steadily.

Mom and I got on each side of him and walked him to the car. I opened the car door and he kind of fell back into the front seat. I handed him the seatbelt and he drew it over his small frame. I heard it click. I shut the door, then slid into the back.

"Any mail today?" I asked Mom.

"Yep," Pop said. "Moravian cookies from Hazel."

"Anything else?" I asked. I looked at mom in the rearview mirror. She shook her head.

"Sunshine and rainbows," Pop said brightly. That's how Hazel always signed her cards.

I rolled my eyes. I looked out the window. I watched Person Street become Atlantic. The houses along the street gave way to businesses. Salvation Army. Gables Motor Lodge. Family Circus Restaurant. Fabric World. Econo Auto Repair.

It was silly to think anyone would write back.

I looked at the back of Pop's head.

As if she could hear me thinking, my mom echoed Pop. "Sunshine and rainbows, Aidan!"

I had no business feeling sorry for myself. I leaned up between the two front seats. "How're you doing, Pop?" "Any day you're alive is a good day, my grandson," he responded.

I looked out the window. There wasn't anything else to say.

Mom turned onto Whitaker Mill.

"Parking lot's full," I pointed to Snoopy's.

"It's worth the wait," Pop said.

I nodded. Some things are definitely worth the wait.

Cleveland Clinic

Delos M. Cosgrove, MD
Chief Executive Officer and President

June 24, 2014

Aidan Colvin

Dear Aidan:

Thank you very much for your note. Dyslexia is an advantage in the fact that it makes us think more creatively. I have enclosed a book that I think you will enjoy. It speaks of my journey on page 362. Hard work will get you there Aidan.

Sincerely,

Delos M. Cosgrove, MD
Chief Executive Officer
and President

DMC/aj

6 THE FIRST LETTER

The next day, Dr. Spiritos confirmed that Pop's cancer had come back. He was going to try another course of chemo.

I was out mowing the lawn, when Mom called out the back door, "Package!"

I cut the motor.

"What?" I said. I shielded my eyes from the sun.

"Package," she repeated. She held it out to me.

I ran up the back steps and grabbed the yellow padded envelope she was holding. It was heavy. I turned it over.

The envelope was too fat to fit in the mailbox so the mailman had rung the bell. The return address said "DM Cosgrove. The Cleveland Clinic."

"Oh, my God," I said. "I think someone wrote back!" DM Cosgrove was a surgeon. He was also President of the Cleveland Clinic.

I put the package on the dining room table and ran to the kitchen to get a knife.

"Oh my God. Oh my God, oh my God," I muttered to myself.

My mom followed me. I didn't want to tear anything that might be inside. I carefully slit the envelope open.

A thick book, *Overcoming Dyslexia: A New Complete Science-Based Program for Reading Problems At Any Level,* by Dr. Sally Shaywitz fell out along with a typed letter on Cleveland Clinic stationary.

I picked up the book and looked at it.

My mom was impatient. "What does the letter say?"

"Wait a minute," I said, slowly.

The cover letter was short and to the point.

I scanned it and passed it, on to Mom. She read it. "Wow," she said.

Yeah, wow, I thought. Someone had replied.

And not just someone.

The Chief Executive Officer and President of the Cleveland Clinic had replied.

I started singing, "Because I'm happy...Clap along if you feel like a room without a roof... Because I'm happy..."

"What are you doing?" my mom smiled.

"The happy dance," I said. I grabbed her hands and pulled her into the den.

I stopped to read the letter again.

Dr. Cosgrove said, "Dyslexia is an advantage in that it makes us think more creatively."

What did he mean? I carefully folded the letter up and slid it into the book.

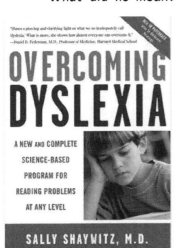

"I got to start dinner," Mom said, turning towards the kitchen. "Are you finished with the yard?"

"Almost," I said.

I suddenly remembered a project I did on the Civil War in eighth grade. We were supposed to write a paper on what it was like to be out on the battlefield. I asked the teacher if I could make a movie instead. She hesitated. I begged. She said, "as long as you meet the requirements."

I wrote, starred in, shot and edited a live news report from the battlefield.

My teacher watched it. I saw her show it to another teacher. She showed it to our whole class. "Great job," she said to me.

Is that what Dr. Cosgrove meant? I never would have

suggested shooting a movie if I didn't have so much trouble writing.

"Did you finish the lawn?" Mom asked again.

"I will," I said. "But first I want to look at this." I held up Dr. Shaywitz's book.

Mom looked at me over her glasses. It's not something I usually say. All right, it's not something I ever say.

Mom went back to chopping. I ran up the stairs two at a time to my room and closed the door. I opened the book.

Inside it said that Dr. Shaywitz and her husband studied dyslexia. They founded The Yale Center for Creativity and Dyslexia. Creativity and Dyslexia?

I flipped to page 362. Dr. Cosgrove said that he had always wanted to be a doctor. He had worked hard in college just to get into medical school.

"While everyone else was partying or going to the movies or sports events, I packed my suitcase and left campus for home where I studied all weekend."

Dr. Cosgrove had meant what he said to me, "Hard work will get you there."

I'd hoped he'd tell me some shortcut, some secret that would make my dyslexia kind of melt away, like the radiation did to Pop's tumors.

AIDAN'S TIP

Yes, it really is called The Yale Center for Creativity and Dyslexia. And if you haven't looked it up, you need to right now. Especially if you're having one of those "I'm a total loser" days." In our house, when I have those, my dad pretends he's Rocky's coach during the final fight scene where you think Rocky's about to die. "Come on, champ!" he says. "Back in the ring..." It doesn't always make me feel better, but it can make me laugh. The Yale website has a lot of great stories about people with dyslexia.

If anyone could, Dr. Cosgrove could. Right?

Instead, he was telling me there wasn't a secret.

I kicked my desk.

I was working hard. I was working so fricking hard. I was studying easily twice as long as my friends. I was still making lower grades. I'd never get into medical school, not that I wanted to. But I was starting to wonder if I'd ever even get into college.

I stood up and walked over to the window.

I returned to my bed and started reading again.

Dr. Cosgrove confessed that he had applied to thirteen medical schools. Only one had accepted him.

"That's all I needed," he said, "just one."

I lay back down on my bed and stared up at the ceiling.

I closed the book. I looked at his letter again.

"Hard work will get you there, Aidan."

I wandered back downstairs. Mom was in the kitchen, slicing homemade pasta into strips with a pizza cutter.

I watched her wiggle a spatula under the floury strips of dough, then drop them into the pot of boiling water on the stove. She looked up.

"I can't believe he wrote," she said.

"Yeah," I said.

"What's the matter?" she asked.

"I'm not like him," I said.

She interrupted me, "maybe..."

"No," I said.

She went on, "maybe...you just don't know it yet." She pulled another ball of dough from the bowl and began to knead it into a thick round disk.

I didn't say anything.

She sprinkled flour on the counter, plopped the disk down and rolled it out.

"Set the table," she commanded, continuing to slice the dough into narrow strips.

"Okay." I grabbed a stack of plates and walked into the dining room. I set six places. I put a napkin and a water glass at each place.

I got a response. My first response.

If I was honest I hadn't expected any.

Maybe I was on to something?

Dr. Cosgrove's path felt like it was in a different universe. But that didn't mean his advice didn't apply to me.

"Hard work will get you there, Aidan."

I went up to my room and tacked his letter on the bulletin board over my desk.

"Dinner," Mom called from downstairs. "Aidan, can you get Pop?"

"Yep!" I ran downstairs to Pop's room. His eyes were closed. I stood there and watched him for a moment. He suddenly looked so much older.

I gently shook his shoulder. "You awake, Pop?" I said.

He opened his eyes. He looked confused for a moment.

"Dinner time," I said.

He sat up and swung his legs off the bed. I leaned over and gave him my arm.

"Thanks, my grandson," he said, taking it. And we walked back to the dining room together where the rest of the family was waiting.

"Who's going to say the blessing?" Dad asked.

"I will," I said. We all bowed our heads. "Thank you for this delicious meal and for Dr. Cosgrove's letter," I said. I glanced over at Pop. "And for letting us all be together."

"Amen," said Pop.

"Amen," everyone said.

"Dig in," said Mom. And we all did.

> Dyslexia is a strength in that it makes you think more creatively... Hard work will get you there.
> — Dr. Delos Cosgrove

7 DREAMS

Last night I dreamed Jay Leno had invited me onto The Tonight Show. I know. I know he's retired from the show, but he's still doing standup. In fact, he's performing in North Carolina next spring.

Anyway, I was backstage when I heard him say, "And welcome.... Aaaaaaaai-dan Colvin." The producer nudged me forward and I strode into the spotlight in my natty suit, Sperry's and a red bowtie.

The auditorium was packed, the applause deafening. But I wasn't nervous. I was "in the zone." Eye of the tiger, baby. I waved to the audience and shielded my eyes against the lights. I walked back and forth. They kept clapping. I saw my parents and my little sisters stand up and wave to me. I waved back. The audience was going wild.

Jay waited for it to calm down, then walked across the stage to shake my hand. He held onto it for a moment longer than necessary and pulled me up to him. We compared heights.

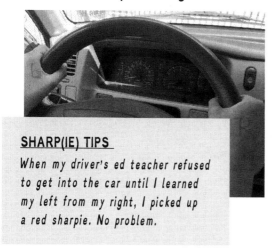

"Are you really fifteen?" he asked.

I nodded.

"Driving?" he asked.

"Not well," I said.

"Can you see over the wheel?" he asked.

"Not exactly," I said, "but being short's not all bad.

I mimed the benefits during a high school

SHARP(IE) TIPS

When my driver's ed teacher refused to get into the car until I learned my left from my right, I picked up a red sharpie. No problem.

slow dance. The audience laughed.

Jay told the audience that he'd invited me on not for my quick wit, but because of my book about dyslexic heroes. He told the audience how he had found me hiding in his bushes one morning when going out to get the paper.

He was in his underwear. I had a camera.

"Showed tenacity," he said. The audience chuckled.

Leno mentioned to the audience that I had written him because he was dyslexic, too. He said he had hated school. He was always cutting up and getting in trouble. In fact, his fifth grade teacher wrote on his report card, "If Jay spent as much time studying as he does trying to be a comedian, he'd be a big star."

Everyone laughed.

Then Jay leaned forward and asked me to tell the audience how my project got started.

I strode out into the spotlight. I raised my arms and looked out into the audience.

Then I felt something cold slide down my shirt. I opened my eyes. My sister Livia was smiling deviously down at me.

"Geez!" I jumped up, shaking my shirt. Four cubes fell to the floor.

"Livia!" I yelled.

"Time to get up," she said sweetly.

"You've got orthodontist," she said.

"Mom!" I yelled.

"And a letter..." She held a white envelope up over her head.

"Give it," I said, trying to grab it.

She backed away.

I lunged again. "Mo---om!"

She dropped it and ran out the door.

Liv yelled, "He's up!"

The envelope was addressed to Ozzy Osbourne. The yellow label on the front said, "Return to Sender."

"Crap." I rubbed my eyes.

Bummer. That was the only address I had found for him.

I went to the bathroom and splashed water on my face. I went back to my room and looked at the envelope again.

Crap, crap, crap.

"Aidan?!" Mom yelled from downstairs, "Ready?"

"Coming," I mumbled.

"Brush your teeth," she yelled.

I didn't answer. I'd sent out twenty letters and gotten two back. One success. One failure.

I looked at Dr. Cosgrove's letter on my bulletin board. I remembered his story about getting all those rejections from medical schools.

That might happen with this project, I thought. Well, I said to myself, if it did I could take one of two tacts: I could quit and forget about it. Or I could brush it off and just send out more letters.

I looked down at the returned letter again. I turned it over in my hands. I opened my desk drawer and shoved the envelope into the back of it.

I decided I was going to send out more.

I pulled on a "Chicago Bulls" t-shirt, grabbed my shoes and ran downstairs.

Mom was waiting.

"Ready?" she asked.

"Yes," I said.

And I was.

AIDAN'S TIP

Revenge is a dish best served cold. Here are tried and true methods to dish it back to bothersome sisters:

- *Make a pile of pretend dog poo (hot cocoa mix and leftover cream of wheat works) and put right where they step when they get out of bed.*
- *Draw a mustache on them while sleeping (permanent ink works best)*
- *Put shaving cream on their hand, then tickle their nose.*
- *Put their hand in warm water (makes them pee)*
- *Post pictures of all of the above on their Instagram account, then on your Instagram, comment on their photos.*

8 FAKE IT TIL YOU MAKE IT

Have you ever noticed how when you start paying attention to one thing, you suddenly see it everywhere? Like when we first got our dogs, Annie and Max. I'd never noticed that many dachshunds before, but then, well, it seemed like everyone had them.

And this project. I didn't know there were so many dyslexics. Now I was starting to see them everywhere. Did you know the guy who designed the shimmer wall on the Raleigh Civic Center is dyslexic? So is this poet my mom's cousin loves. And then earlier today I saw a magazine at the grocery store. The cover article was, "The Advantages of Dyslexia." It was written by a dyslexic astrophysicist at Harvard. I don't even know what an astrophysicist is. But it sounds important.

How could I not have seen these people before? I added their names to my list. I looked them up online, read a bit about them, and found their addresses. Then I dropped a letter to each of them in the mail. I still haven't heard from anyone besides Dr. Cosgrove, but... well... that's okay.

There's a lot of noise in our house these days. Dad and Pop are turning a little bathroom and closet upstairs into a room for Liv. She's been sharing a room with Sarah. Well, Pop is a little too weak to help, but he's strong enough to shout out commands from his chair. Dad's doing a little shouting of his own. Bleep-da-bleepitty-beep.

Our neighborhood is, as they say, "turning." You know, people are moving in and fixing up houses. That's what we're doing. The house next door is still a boarding house. But our neighbors on the other side, Tina and Mike, are fixing up their house, too.

Even though he's sick, Pop just can't seem to sit still. Last week, he re-varnished an old oak table he built us. He sharpened our kitchen knives. He got Mom to pick up some oak logs left beside the road. He wants to make bowls out of them on his lathe back in Wilmington.

Our family hasn't always lived in Raleigh. I was born in San Francisco. My sister, Livia, was, too. I don't remember much about it. My dad went to school out there. When he graduated, we moved back here to be closer to both sets of grandparents.

Sarah, my youngest sister, was born here. She was born in the hospital where my dad works. Mom says right after Sarah was born, Dad invited all his coworkers into the delivery room to see the baby. Mom was naked. Dad doesn't remember that. Mom'll never forget it.

Mom? She's tough. She keeps us on the straight and narrow. She writes and teaches. And takes care of us and my granddad.

And that's my family, except for Max and Annie, our two not-so-miniature, miniature dachshunds. My little sister Sarah is always dressing them up.

Anyway... I was upstairs whittling when my mom yelled up, "Mail!"

I jumped up and ran downstairs. She held it out to me.

"Ted Turner?" I read in the top left corner.

"Ted Turner?" she echoed.

TURNER ENTERPRISES, INC.

R.E. TURNER
Chairman

June 30, 2014

Mr. Aidan Colvin

Dear Mr. Colvin:

Thank you for your letter of June 19th.

Unfortunately, I am not qualified to discuss Dyslexia with you, because I have never been diagnosed with the condition. It has been incorrectly reported that I have had to overcome Dyslexia, but I simply have no such experiences to share. Let me encourage you to keep running those marathons and playing practical jokes on your sisters.

Thank you for writing, Aidan, and I wish you all the best.

Sincerely,

"He founded **CNN**," I said, fumbling with the envelope. "He's like a billionaire, Mom."

"Oh," she said, staying beside me.

I opened and scanned the letter.

"What does he say?" Mom asked.

"That he's not dyslexic," I said.

She was silent.

I was disappointed.

"He wrote back..." Mom tried to comfort me.

"Yeah," I said, half-heartedly. "Probably won't hear from anyone else."

I clomped back up to my room and closed the door.

I looked at the letter again.

"Keep running those marathons," he had said.

I had enclosed an article I had written about running a half marathon. Even though Turner's not dyslexic, at least he had still read my letter.

. . .

Running that half marathon was a big deal to me. I had decided to run it one night while Mom and I were on a dog walk a couple of years ago. I told her I was nervous about high school. I told her I wanted to do something that would make me feel stronger, something that would distinguish me somehow.

"A half marathon, Aidan?" she had said. "That's over 13 miles."

"I know," I had said. I'd never run over five.

"You need to talk to the coach," she had said.

At the time, I was running in an afterschool program. Mostly short distances. The occasional 5k. I wasn't the fastest, but I was steady.

On Tuesday, I went to practice early so I could talk to Coach Shea alone. She was setting up trail markers. I ran down to help. I told her what I wanted to do.

She quickly said no.

No?

She said I hadn't hit puberty. (Would I ever?) She said this much training could stunt my growth. She said, "Aidan, your body's not made for it. Kids your age run short distances. Fast." She added, "Training for something like that could be," she paused, "damaging."

We both just stood there. I started kicking rocks.

Then she looked directly at me and became really serious. "Aidan..." she said.

I looked up.

"I'll support you on two conditions."

I listened.

"First, you not run another half until you finish growing." She paused. "Until your growth plates close."

I didn't say anything.

"And second..." she started.

"Yeah?"

She looked at me. "A half marathon is tough. A lot of people can get up to seven, eight, nine miles. But you get to ten, eleven, twelve. Then your body gives out...."

I interrupted her. "What's the second condition?"

"Second," she started again, "when you cross that finish line, I want you to know that anything— anything— you set your mind to do, you can do."

We both just stood there. She was watching me. Some kids started jogging towards us. She raised her eyebrows.

"Promise!" I said. Then, I sprinted over to join the group.

"One loop through the forest!" she yelled. And we all took off.

That night, Mom, Aunt Sherri, Uncle Gary and I registered for the Quintiles Half Marathon in Wilmington. It was three months away. Gary, who had been a runner in college, suggested we follow Hal Higdon's Program. He also sent me a link to a video called "Why We Fall."

I put the training program up on the fridge. Then I watched the video. It began, "Life isn't about how hard

Hal Higdon's
Half Marathon Training Program

Half Marathon Training: Novice

Week	Mon	Tue	Wed	Thu	Fri	Sat	Sun
1	Stretch & Strengthen	3 m run	2 m run or cross	3 m run + strength	Rest	30 min cross	4 m run
2	Stretch & Strengthen	3 m run	2 m run or cross	3 m run + strength	Rest	30 min cross	4 m run
3	Stretch & Strengthen	3.5 m run	2 m run or cross	3.5 m run + strength	Rest	40 min cross	5 m run
4	Stretch & Strengthen	3.5 m run	2 m run or cross	3.5 m run + strength	Rest	40 min cross	5 m run
5	Stretch & Strengthen	4 m run	2 m run or cross	4 m run + strength	Rest	40 min cross	6 m run
6	Stretch & Strengthen	4 m run	2 m run or cross	4 m run + strength	Rest or easy run	Rest	5-K Race
7	Stretch & Strengthen	4.5 m run	3 m run or cross	4.5 m run + strength	Rest	50 min cross	7 m run
8	Stretch & Strengthen	4.5 m run	3 m run or cross	4.5 m run	Rest	50 min cross	8 m run
9	Stretch & Strengthen	5 m run	3 m run or cross	5 m run + strength	Rest or easy run	Rest	10-K Race
10	Stretch & Strengthen	5 m run	3 m run or cross	5 m run + strength	Rest	60 min cross	9 m run
11	Stretch & Strengthen	5 m run	3 m run or cross	5 m run + strength	Rest	60 min cross	10 m run
12	Stretch & Strengthen	4 m run	3 m run or cross	2 m run	Rest	Rest	Half Marathon

you hit. It's about how hard you get hit and keep moving forward..." I've watched that video probably a hundred times. It's not just for runners.

That winter, North Carolina set records for snow and ice. School was canceled for almost three weeks. But Mom and I headed out anyway—almost everyday.

It seems like all I did that winter was go to school, run, eat, do homework, eat more and sleep. I was tired all the time. But we logged the miles. We put our weekly totals up on the fridge. We crossed the days off until the race.

The night before the race, we went to bed at 9 pm. We had to get up at 4 am to catch the shuttle to the start line. It was dark, cold and damp. We jogged in place to keep warm.

Uncle Gary and I made our way up to the 6 to 7-minute mile pace group. Mom and Sherri held back to run with the 9-10 minute group. A gunshot fired. And we were off.

The sun was just coming up. The air was cool. I took off at an easy lope with Gary. About mile five, I moved ahead of him. I waved. He grunted. For the next five miles, I'd spot the back of someone I wanted to catch up with and steadily make my way up and pass them. And then pass another person. And another. I grabbed Gatorade at every station.

Around Mile 12, I started running out of gas. I remembered the video Gary sent me. "Pain is temporary. It may last for a minute or an hour or a year, but eventually, it will subside, and something else will take its place. If I quit, however, it will last forever."

I couldn't feel my legs. People were cheering. "Come on, kid! You can do it."

I started to feel dizzy. I saw that a lot of people had stopped to walk. There was a light drizzle and up ahead someone had slipped on the grate of one of the bridges. She was lying on the grass while an EMT delicately lifted her leg.

I watched the backs of other runners in front of me. My lungs hurt. I could see Mayfair Shopping Center ahead. And Mile Marker 13. God, I wanted to walk. Where was the end? I remembered what Coach Shea had said. I tried to distract myself by reading the signs people were holding up.

"Smile if you're not wearing underwear."

"Run like you stole something."

"Kick some asphalt."

"Almost there," someone shouted from the sidelines. "A quarter of a mile."

A quarter mile? I could hear the faint calls and whistles from the finish line.

"Look at that kid," someone yelled. I looked around. I realized they were talking about me. I had a surge of energy. I took off.

"Go, Aidan!" I heard Livia running along beside me. "Go! Go!"

Dad was holding Sarah under a poncho at the finish line. "Yeah, Aidan!" he and Sarah screamed.

And then I was done. A woman slid the half marathon medal over my head. Someone else handed me a Gatorade and Pop put a blanket over my shoulders.

I had done it. I had really done it.

. . .

I stared back at Ted Turner's letter now. I sat down at my desk. I pulled out the returned envelope from Ozzie Osbourne. I looked at both of them.

It was disappointing, but Ted Turner did write back. At least the letter seemed to have a real signature on it. I held it up to the light and studied it. If it was a stamp it was pretty convincing. Not like those obvious stamped signatures where the ink runs out or globs up in the middle of the line or something.

I reread his letter. He told me to keep running.

Running the half marathon had been good for me.

I'd felt strong, proud. I wear that race shirt all the time. (In fact, I'm wearing it right now.)

Funny. When I sent out the first twenty letters, I had really low expectations. I mean who takes the time to write back to a kid they don't know? It was like throwing a handful of seeds into the wind.

I remembered preparing for the half marathon. I saw, week after week, that the miles added up.

Maybe if I kept sending out letters, the responses would, too?

So what if Ted Turner wasn't dyslexic? He had written back. Dr. Cosgrove had, too... They were both super successful. Just having their letters in front of me... I mean, if they believed in me... well...

I tacked Ted Turner's letter up next to Dr. Cosgrove's. I plugged in my headphones and navigated to my half marathon playlist. The first song was "Born to Run" by Bruce Springsteen.

Did you know that he was dyslexic?

I can't confirm it, but I'm going to write him. In fact, that is who I'm writing to right now.

Keep running. — Ted Turner

9 ARMING ONESELF

"Come here, Sarah." Pop was sitting on a stool in our family room. He had fastened his haircloth on and was rummaging through his red toolbox of clippers down by his feet. He pulled some scissors out and handed them to her.

"Really?" Sarah asked.

"It's going to fall out anyway," Pop said. The cancer had come back. He was going to start chemo again tomorrow.

He reached into his toolbox again and pulled out an electric shaver and handed it to Liv. She plugged it in. It made a high-pitched thrumming noise.

"Careful!" Mom said.

"Leave me some!" Sarah said to Liv.

"I will," Liv said.

"Aidan, make sure they don't cut him," Mom said, going back to chopping onions.

I nodded, while eating a lollipop.

Dad walked in with a pile of mail, which he was absent-mindedly flipping through. "One for me. Two for

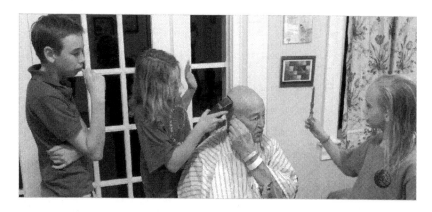

Mom. One for you," he said, handing me an envelope. "Two for me. One for Max... "

Our dachshund Max looked up. Sarah cooed, "Little Max-y..."

Dad tossed an envelope next to Max, "Pre-approved for a credit card, I see..."

Livia went back to shaving.

"They'll approve anybody these days," Pop said. Then, folding down his right ear, he said, "Make sure you get behind the ears." White fuzz was falling off in clumps.

I looked at the envelope he had tossed me. It had a royal crest on it.

"Buckingham Palace?" I read, incredulously.

Sarah didn't take her eyes off Liv, who was proceeding to shave Pop's neck. "What?"

"BUCKINGHAM Palace," I repeated. "Buckingham PALACE," I said again, for emphasis.

Livia turned off the clippers.

The round stamp indicated it had in fact been mailed from Buckingham Palace just five days earlier. It was marked "Royal Mail."

Pop brushed the loose hair off his forehead and eyes. Sarah blew fine hairs off his cheeks.

"Use the brush," Pop said. Livia rummaged through the red steel box. She handed Sarah the brush. Sarah brushed his neck and face.

I gently tore open the envelope and pulled out the letter. The left-hand corner had a coat of arms. It was inscribed "Honi Soit Qui Mal Y Pense." I showed Dad. "Latin," Dad translated. "'Shame be to him who thinks evil.'" He raised and lowered his bushy eyebrows menacingly.

The letter was from Amanda Thirsk, Private Secretary to The Duchess of York. (If you don't follow the royal family, that's Princess Beatrice, Queen Elizabeth's granddaughter.)

"Aidan Colvin, Esquire," I read.

"Apprentice to a knight," Dad translated again. Livia looked at him disbelievingly. He tapped his forehead. My dad really is a font of odd trivia.

25th June, 2014

Dear Aidan,

       Princess Beatrice of York has asked me to thank you for your letter dated 19th June, 2014. As you know, Her Royal Highness also has dyslexia. Princess Beatrice has been very fortunate in the support she has received from a wide variety of people. They have enabled her to overcome her dyslexia. Her Royal Highness is confident that you too can do so and wishes you every success with your time at school.

       Princess Beatrice sends you and your family her very best wishes

Yours sincerely,

Amanda Thirsk

Amanda Thirsk LVO
Private Secretary to The Duke of York

Aidan Colvin, Esq.

I had written to Princess Beatrice because I had seen her in the news. She was visiting a school for kids with dyslexia. In the caption below her photo, it had said she was dyslexic.

"Let me see that," Pop said.

I handed him the envelope. He put his glasses on.

"Buckingham Palace," he read, slowly, disbelievingly. He closed his eyes and said to Sarah, "you missed some." She brushed the fine hairs off his forehead and cheeks.

"It's a different time, Aidan," Pop said, returning the envelope to me.

He looked at Liv and Sarah. "How do I look?"

"Great!" they said.

"Read it aloud," Mom said.

I started to read the letter. Ms. Thirsk said Princess Beatrice had a wide variety of people support her.

I wondered if it's easier to have dyslexia in England. Maybe. If you're a princess, everything's probably a little easier.

In the article, Princess Beatrice had said that wanting to read Harry Potter was what motivated her to learn.

God, I had just wanted to be able to read. Period. Harry Potter was so far beyond me when my friends were reading it. The first books I "read" were graphic novels... Superman, Batman, Star Wars... I could at least read the pictures. I guess the first real chapter book I read was Captain Underpants. Not exactly princess material.

Ms. Thirsk said the Duke of York had "overcome" her dyslexia and she was confident that I could, too.

Overcome? Dr. Shaywitz who wrote the book Dr. Cosgrove sent, said you never outgrow dyslexia.

Maybe what Ms. Thirsk had meant was that Princess Beatrice had learned to cope with it.

Or maybe even use it.

After all, Dr. Cosgrove said it forces you to think

more creatively. See things that others don't see.

I think that that's true. At least for other people.

But for me? I don't know.

What I do know is that this project is leading me places I wouldn't have found if I had just stayed on the sidelines, waiting for a knight in shining armor to show up. Instead I'm arming myself.

And look who has showed up so far.

A princess.

A princess, a surgeon and a billionaire.

Her Royal Highness is confident that you, too, can do so (overcome dyslexia) and wishes you every success with your time in school.
— Amanda Thirsk

Date: 6/30/14

Name: Diane C Swonk

Profession: Economist

Who was your hero as a kid and why?
Mary Tyler Moore — she had a television series that showed women could reach for their dreams and make a difference. My parents were also very involved in the civil rights movement, and I thought Martin Luther King was a hero; it also made me see how ugly things could be when I was young.

Many dyslexics don't succeed, but you did. Can you point to someone or something that helped you become the success you are?
I had a very lonely childhood; if I didn't figure out how to do things on my own, I feared no one would notice. My parents are also both dyslexic, and they hid it from my teachers. I was expected to do well no matter what. Thankfully, I had one teacher who taught me to take notes. She helped me use those skills to compensate for my challenges reading.

Do you have a story from your life that might help me or others stay hopeful and keep trying when we've had a challenging setback because of the dyslexia?
I wish I could be inspirational. I know that my dyslexia allowed me to think outside of the box — look at problems from a different perspective, and see outcomes others couldn't. I also believe (know) success is a process of learning from failures.

What one piece of advice or wisdom would you give to a dyslexic kid today?
Never give up: it is our differences not our similarities that define us. Embrace who you are. Never run from it. I had got me more through learning college experiences and through my graduate school. My notes were meticulous.

It literally got me through learning college experiences and through my graduate school. My notes were meticulous

May I contact you directly if I have an additional question? If so, will you give me a phone number or email I can use? (I will not share it with anyone.)

Thank you!

10 LOOKING FOR ONE THING, FINDING ANOTHER

All right. If this were a movie, the camera would start wide angle to show my mom sticking her head into my room and me asleep in bed. As soon as she closes the door, in Ferris Buehler fashion, the camera would zoom in tight and I'd whisper conspiratorially, "So, how does an unknown kid like me get the attention of someone like Jay Leno? Ideas? Anyone? Anyone? Buehler?"

But this is not a movie. There are no cameras. It's just me. Alone. Here in bed, trying to think. Come on, brain! Think!

Maybe I should try one of those energy drinks like Monster or Kickstart or Redbull? Or go shoot some baskets or jump in the shower? Sometimes I get good ideas there--if I'm not interrupted. See, we all share one bathroom. No locks. My sisters are always walking in. Mom knocked on my door.

"Busy?" she asked, pushing it open. She was holding an envelope. She read the name in the top left-hand corner. "Diane Swonk? Is that how you say it? S-w-o-n-k?" she said slowly.

I stared at her for a minute, still thinking about Leno, then I jumped up. "Let me see." I walked over to look.

She handed it to me. The envelope was thick. I opened one end and pulled the pages out. Ms. Swonk had sent, gosh, one, two, three, four pages.

"Who is she?" Mom asked.

"An economist," I answered. "I've seen her on the news."

Ms. Swonk had written in cursive.

"I can't read it," I winced. "Can you?" I handed it to her.

She took it and began.

Diane was the first person who had taken the time to not just write, but to answer my four questions. She said one of her heroes was Mary Tyler Moore because she showed that women could reach for their dreams.

Maybe that's what I was trying to do with this project? Show dyslexic kids that they, too, could reach for theirs?

"Are you listening?" Mom interrupted.

"Yes!" I nodded. I was putting together Legos on my bed. "I'm always listening."

"I hate it when you're doing something else while I'm reading," she said.

"It helps me concentrate," I said. It does. I pushed the Legos away anyway and leaned back on my pillow.

Mom started reading again. "I had a very lonely childhood..."

I sat up. No one had said that yet. Diane had a lonely childhood? I'm still lonely.

I do have a couple good friends. Levi. Julia. Max. Anna, Joey...

Am I lonely because of the dyslexia? Not entirely, but it is a piece of it.

I mean you get separated at school from friends early on. Smart kids here, not so smart there.

AIDAN'S TIP

Charter and specialized public schools tend to be smaller—which, for me, means that the teachers tend to be less maxed out and have more time to help. I moved to a STEM (science/ technology/ engineering/ math) high school this year not because I like those subjects, but because the school is small and there is a lot of support. It's also a lot closer to home than where I was going before.

And then I bounced around, trying to find the right school. In Raleigh, we have regular schools, magnet schools and charter schools. Those are all public. And then, of course, private schools. I've gone to five schools. Four public and one private. This fall, I'm moving to my sixth. Most of my friends have gone to school with the same kids since kindergarten. Every time I've moved, it's an entirely new group of kids.

Mom stopped reading for a second to take a sip of tea.

"I'm listening," I said, impatiently. I showed her my hands were empty.

She put her cup down and continued.

Ms. Swonk said it wasn't until a teacher stepped in and helped her learn how to take notes that she turned her school work around.

I can't even imagine being a good note-taker. If the teacher is talking and I try to take notes, I get lost trying to spell words and then, when I turn back to listening, I've missed so much content that I'm utterly lost. If I try to type my notes, the spellchecker invariably replaces misspelled words with other words.

Mom read on, "I wish I could be inspirational. I know that my dyslexia allowed me to think outside of the box— look at problems from a different perspective and see outcomes others couldn't."

That's kind of what Dr. Cosgrove said, I thought.

I could hear Pop's cane tapping the floor below. He yelled up the stairs. "How's my favorite grandson?"

I yelled back, "I'm your only grandson."

"You want to get a burger at The Station?" he called.

"In a minute," I yelled back.

"I'll be on the porch," he said.

Mom looked at me. I nodded for her to keep reading. She searched for her place, then continued,

"I also believe success is a process of learning from failures."

Learning from failures. Learning from failures?

I thought about it for a minute.

I'd had a lot of failures. A lot.

Mostly related to school.

What happens after I fail something?

If it's because I didn't understand it, I double up on studying. Go to afterschool tutoring or SMART lunch. But if it's something related to the dyslexia—like misspelling place names on a map— we'd see if there was a work-around. Sometimes we'd make an adjustment to my IEP.

You know what an IEP is, right?

It's not a radical Islamic terrorist group or brand of deodorant. It stands for "Individualized Educational Plan." I used to cringe when people found out I had one. I was embarrassed. But let me tell you, if you've got a big learning "difference," it's much better to be upfront about it than act like you don't.

AIDAN'S IEP

- *I get a silent environment for tests*
- *I dictate all written work*
- *I get teacher or student notes*
- *For some essay tests, I dictate my answers to a teacher*
- *I get extended time on tests and some assignments.*
- *For bubble tests, I answer in the booklet and someone else transfers them to the bubble sheets.*
- *I get a Starbucks Grande Hot Chocolate with Whipped Cream and sprinkles (well, that's in my dreams).*

Diane said that success is a process of learning from failures. My failures have sometimes led to changes in my IEP. For example, I used to bomb all standardized tests, even if I knew the content. (And by failing, I mean scoring in the seventeenth percentile, not the seventieth). One reason was that I have a hard time tracking from the end of the question to the line of bubble answers. I'm also super slow. My scores went up quite a bit (like fifty points) when I started getting time and a half and when I circled my answers in the test booklet and someone else transferred them to the bubble sheet.

Anyway, my point is that an IEP is not something you should avoid because you don't want people to know you're different. It's something you should absolutely get in place so that you can convey the things you do know. Take a look at the grey box to see what is on my high school IEP.

As for Diane's point about learning from failures... It's painful to fail. I know. Especially in the high stress fishbowl of high school. Like Diane, I've had to learn from my failures.

Do I feel like giving up at times?

Yeah. Like last week.

My history teacher, Mr. Bagwell, asked me to come see him during lunch. It was about a paper I had dictated. I got a D. I was mortified when he pointed out some of the mistakes, like this one. I had meant to write "America's busy factories..." but dictation heard something else.

conomic Growth and the Early Industrial Revolution 1790s- 1830s
conomical growth in the early industrial revolution was crucial in creating a backbone
or America today. This is seen as how we have a service-based economy and how we
as a nation have strived to industrialize ourselves constantly and create one of the most
stable governments in the world.

Examples

The First American Factories 1793
The first American factory really shaped how America's pussy factories and
industrialization today even though many ways two jobs and warred factories have been

What to do?
Give up?

Not if I want to graduate.

Diane would said, "Learn from your failures."

I know I'll certainly have my computer read what I've dictated back to me, when possible, from now on.

Mom continued to read Diane's letter aloud.

"Never give up. It is our differences, not our similarities, that define us."

I noticed Mom's eyes were getting watery. My mom is a crier.

"Are you crying?" I grimaced.

"No." She said, defensively. She read on,

"Embrace who you are. Never run from it."

We were both quiet.

If this were a movie, this is when the harp music would fade on. Mom would put the letter down and put her hand on my shoulder. We would look out the window. And there would be... Jay Leno.

In my dreams.

Instead, Mom said, "People have been so kind."

I nodded. I thought of what people had said so far.

"Hard work will get you there."

"What are your strengths? Run with them."

"Embrace who you are."

I shrugged. Mom was right.

> It's our differences rather than our similarities that define us. Embrace who you are. Never run from it.
> — Diane Swonk

11 IMPROVISE

Julia and Levi are probably my best friends. Levi's this giant with a mop of curly blond hair and he's always bouncing around, like a pogo stick. And Julia's not your typical girl. I mean, she's the only person I know who has a second-degree full-fledged black belt. No joke. She could kick my butt. I know that's not saying a whole lot, but I think you know what I mean.

I've known them both since sixth grade. They're the kind of friends you can say anything to.

In middle school, we had a funny class called "Wellness," where we'd sit in a circle and talk about our feelings. It was hokey. We still joke about it.

"How are you feeling today, Levi?" I asked. We were over at Levi's house after getting a concrete at Goodberry's at Cameron Village. It's a 32-ounce custard milkshake that feels like concrete in your stomach if you drink the whole thing.

"How are you feeling..." Levi asked and fired a round of nerf bullets at me. "Now?"

"Stop!" I said, covering myself. I clutched my stomach. "I'm going to vomit."

"Better not," Levi said, firing another round.

"Try me," I warned. I doubled over and started to loudly wretch. Levi hates vomit. That's actually an understatement. He put his nerf gun down.

"Trashcan?" he handed it to me.

I lunged for his gun. Julia started firing. I joined in.

"No fair!" He said. He tried to wrestle it back. Unsuccessfully. "What's your new school look like?" he asked me.

I picked up some of the nerf bullets on the floor. I leaned in to loud-whisper, "It's in a psych ward." I raised my eyebrows, menacingly.

"No!" Julia gasped.

I nodded yes.

"Creepy," Levi said, looking around the basement for another nerf gun.

"Or crazy," I retorted, and shot him in the butt.

"Hey!" he yelled.

I was starting in a few weeks and I knew officially ZERO, yes, Z-E-R-O people. Null. Nada. No one. I'd be the "new kid" again.

I'd hoped to start the school year strong. To have this project under my belt. I'd written almost 100 people now. Some of them twice. A few three times. (Jay Leno, yes, I'm talking to you.)

I thought if I heard from a lot of people, I'd be all set for success.

What had happened was I had heard from some people, but I still felt nervous.

"You'll be fine," Mom said. "You'll find your tribe."

"What are you? Chopped liver?" my dad added.

"Yeah," I nodded. I felt like chopped liver.

Another new school. New teachers, systems, kids. And no fluff. It's a STEM high school. You know — science, technology, engineering, math. Aside from the technology part, it's all the subjects I stink at.

"At least you won't be spending your life on the #105," Mom said.

I'd ridden the bus to Durham and back all last year to

go to a small charter school there. Two to three hours a day on the bus or waiting for it.

I went upstairs and sat down on my bed. I pulled out my lock-picking set. I might not be good at the quadratic equation, but I sure can pick a lock. My record is 42 seconds.

A few minutes later, Mom called upstairs, "Aidan! Another letter!"

"What?"

"Another letter!" she yelled again.

I ran downstairs.

She handed me the envelope. "And you thought no one else would write," she said.

She waited for me to say I was wrong. I didn't. I looked at the return address. "Thomas Sayre. Sayre. Clearscapes. Raleigh..." Thomas Sayre? I thought for a moment. Oh, yeah! The artist and sculptor.

I slit open the envelope and pulled out the sheets. In the cover letter, Mr. Sayre wrote,

"I am honored to have been contacted by you as someone who you think has become successful in some way in spite of or perhaps because of dyslexia. During my life, I have barely spoken about the issue with anyone."

I put the cover letter down and went on to the second page. My mom read over my shoulder.

I turned to block her view.

> ### AIDAN'S TIPS
> *When I'm listening to a book in the Learning Ally player or in Overdrive, I adjust the reading speed to 1.5x speed. When I'm on a website, I highlight text and have the computer read it to me using the screen reader. I also use an application called "PDF reader." To spice things up, I change the computer voice. Right now my iPhone is set to an Australian English Male voice.*

Name: Thomas Sayre
Date: July 7, 2014
Profession: Artist/Sculptor

Who was your hero as a kid and why?

I most definitely did not have one hero as a child. My heroes were heroes of all sorts very broadly defined: artists, some political leaders, and more generally, original thinkers were my heroes. I was not raised to emulate anyone. Rather, I was encouraged to be original. We were taught to see through the facades of want-a-be's. We were taught to question people who held large positions, but who were not making particular contribution from that position. My siblings and I were taught to respect people who are themselves and had the willpower to try to affect the world from that unique position. I had a very positive, though, at times, very difficult upbringing.

Specifically, Martin Luther King was a hero, the musician Dave Brubeck was a hero, my father was a hero, but even more so, my mother was a hero. My swimming coach, who taught me how to weld when I was 15, was also a hero.

Many dyslexics don't succeed, but you did. Can you point to someone or something that helped you become the success you are?

My mother was probably the single biggest reason for my eventual "success in life". She was the first to realize that I had significant problems being in a regular school. She had the wisdom to not send me to the fancy private school which I was "destined" to attend, but rather shipped me off to an experimental school where I met Diana King, who was a very early educator of dyslexics and other reading disabilities. She went on to become quite well known. Most of all, my mother and a few other adults placed value on what might have been called my "eccentric creativity".

As I went off to college, by then an academic success (but not without great effort), my mother stopped me and said: "some day you will have a secretary/helper who will type and spell and, generally, help you put your ideas into words." She was right. Ten years after I went to college, I sent her a letter which had been typed and corrected by a trusted secretary/helper.

Do you have a story from your life that might help me or others stay hopeful and keep trying when we've had a challenging setback because of the dyslexia?

Improbably, I majored in English in college. I loved the ideas, the discourse, the images from poems and novels and plays. What I couldn't do very well and, in fact, disliked was reading. This was particularly challenging in a Shakespeare class. I figured out that at the college library there were LP records of every Shakespeare play. I could play them at 78 rpms and listen to the plays and comprehend them vastly better than reading Elizabethan English. It appears that most dyslexics are improvisers. We have to be.

What one piece of advice or wisdom would you give to a dyslexic kid today?

Be an improviser. Surround yourself with people who believe in you and realize that the skill in reading/spelling/syntax (all the stuff dyslexics are not so good at) is not a sign of intelligence necessarily. Find people who truly prize who you are, what you do or what you want to do, and then you have to work very hard to do that.

Mr. Sayre mentioned Martin Luther King as a hero. Diane Swonk had, too. But he also said "original thinkers."

"Oh, look," Mom said, pointing to the third paragraph, "he said his mom was probably the single biggest reason for his success."

I rolled my eyes.

She smiled. Then she headed out the front door.

I could hear her turning the hose on.

I went back to reading.

Mr. Sayre also talked about loving Shakespeare, but having a lot of trouble reading it. As a work-around, he found records of the plays in the library. He liked listening because he could better understand the language, control the speed of the recording and listen to them over and over and over.

I do that. When I don't understand a lecture at school, I go online (to Crash Course or other websites, if my teacher doesn't have materials online). I use other tools, too, like SparkNotes, Quizlet and Quizzles. And of course, audiobooks.

When Mr. Sayre went off to college, his mom said, "Some day you will have a secretary or assistant who will type and spell and help you put your ideas into words."

Ten years later, Mr. Sayre sent his mom a letter that had been typed by a trusted secretary. She had been right.

It made me remember a docu-mentary called "The Big Picture." In it, billionaire Richard Branson said the same thing. He hired people to do the things he couldn't. So did financial wizard Charles Schwab. And former President George Bush, Jr.

Pop said my grandmother Nana had been his secretary. She had managed the bills and accounting for his barbershop and their household. Not having to do the things that were hardest for him freed him up to do the things he was good at (like talking to his customers or leading the boy scout troop or building furniture). Pop is good at a lot.

So is Mr. Sayre. I wonder how long it took him to realize that. I wonder when I'll find something I feel good at.

One thing Mr. Sayre said that got my attention was,

"It appears that most dyslexics are improvisers. We have to be."

I hadn't thought of it that way, but he's right. I am always having to figure out how to make something work for me. Sometimes I reach for a high tech solution, like dictation. Sometimes it's simple and low tech, like using graph paper to help keep my math calculations in line.

Mr. Sayre also said, "Find people who prize who you are/what you do and what you want to do."

When he was my age, he said he was just learning how to weld — not because it would get him a job, but because it interested him.

> **AIDAN'S LOW-TECH TIPS**
> - Use the edge of colored paper to run under the text I'm reading
> - Use highlighters
> - Translate information into pictures
> - Use graph paper to keep my numbers lined up
> - Make up mnemonics to help you remember information (like the first states)
> - Ask friends if you can take pictures of their notes

Then he kept following the things that interested him until he eventually found himself developing a whole new form of sculpture called "earthcasting." He studies a site and comes up with an idea for that place. He then digs molds out of the earth and pours concrete into them. He lets them harden, then uses heavy equipment to raise and position them.

In this photo, Mr. Sayre is beside one of his projects, called "Gyre," at the **NC** Art Museum.

It occurs to me that I might be doing something similar. I mean I started this project because I was trying to figure out how to work around my learning disability.

But as I've gotten into it, my focus has changed. I'm starting to see that dyslexia might also give you abilities. The people who have written back so far have mentioned big-picture thinking and creativity.

And sure, I know that dyslexia comes with challenges, but maybe that's not only a bad thing. I mean everyone has to learn how to deal with challenges at some point in their lives, right? Who knows? Maybe because us dyslexics have to learn that earlier, that might even be considered a benefit.

(I can't believe I'm saying that.)

Most dyslexics are improvisers. We have to be.
Find people who prize who you are/what you do and
what you want to do, and then you have to work
very hard at that.   — Thomas Sayre

PHOTO CREDIT Jimmy Williams, *Walter Magazine*

12 TRY

"Come on. Just try." Julia was lying on the couch at my house. Levi, Charlotte, Julia and I were playing Mario Cart.

"I don't do sports," Levi said, without looking away from the screen. "I don't like to sweat."

"I'm too small..." I said, carefully watching my car.

"Not to cox," said Charlotte.

Levi said, "Inappropriate language, Charlotte Crouse!"

Charlotte looked at him and rolled her eyes. "It's a position on the boat."

"I'm always picked last," I added, cutting off Julia's car.

"Hey, that wasn't fair," Julia said, eyes glued to the screen.

"What's a cox?" I asked, continuing to drive.

"The person who barks the orders," Charlotte said.

"That'd be perfect for you!" Levi yelled. "Hey, don't kill me!" He madly worked his controller.

I ran him off the track anyway. "Perfect?" I said sarcastically.

"Hey!" Levi said.

I rammed Charlotte and Julia off the track, too.

"World domination!" I jumped up on the coffee table. "Oh, yeah!"

. . .

And that is how I found myself (without Levi) on the fringes of a scraggly group of middle and high school rowers at the Triangle Rowing Club on Lake Wheeler. Everyone was huddled around Coach Will and Coach

Schaffer. The guys who had been rowing for awhile... they were up front. Most weren't wearing shirts. They all had six packs.

I looked down at my stomach. I wouldn't be taking my shirt off.

We started with land practice, eight laps around a hilly loop. Then the more seasoned rowers filed off towards the racks of boats. The rest of us newcomers gathered around Coach Shaffer. We tried to look at ease.

I watched the veterans lift the long, white shells onto their muscular shoulders and carry them, like lines of ants, down to the water.

"How much do you weigh?" Coach Shaffer studied me.

"Ninety. Maybe ninety-two," I said.

"You should cox," Coach Schaffer said, marking her clipboard. "You're in the Queen Anne with Nathan in stroke seat. He'll teach you the commands."

"The Queen Anne?" I said.

She pointed to the boat and I ran to catch it. The boys had just rolled the shell off their shoulders and softly into the water. I slipped out of my Sperrys and left them in the pile of shoes by the dock.

Coach Shaffer yelled down to the group, "Hey, novice boys!"

The boys looked up.

She yelled, "teach Aidan how to cox!"

"Got it, coach," Nathan yelled back.

I stood beside the boat.

"You're there," Nathan said, pointing to the end seat. Before climbing in, he showed me how to put the headgear and mike on and how to turn it on. I climbed into the back. Eight rowers faced me.

Nathan explained starboard and portside and what number each seat was. Then we pushed off.

"Why'd she put me in cox?" I asked him.

"You're small," said Nathan.

"Oh."

"120 is the limit," he added. "You can cox for a couple of years."

For the next two hours, we rowed the periphery of Lake Wheeler. Nathan whispered commands to me and then I barked them out on the mike.

"Louder," the guys up front said.

"Power ten in two!" I yelled. Then I started counting, "One, two, three, four..." The boat shot forward. "Five, six..." I rocked with each stroke. "Seven, eight, nine, TEN!" We flew.

Coach Shaffer motored up beside us. "Nice job, boys. What was the stroke rate, Aidan?"

Nathan pointed to the monitor. "24." (That's 24 strokes per minute.)

"Nice," Coach Shaffer said and sped up to catch the girls' boat ahead of us.

Later that afternoon, after putting up the boats and huddling up to yell "Go, TRC!" (short for Triangle Rowing Club), Mom pulled up in the minivan.

"How was it?" she asked, when I climbed in.

Charlotte and Ann Marie waited for me to answer.

"Awesome," I said.

I thought to myself, it felt like flying.

. . .

After we dropped Charlotte and Ann Marie off, Mom said, "Open the glove compartment." I did. And a postcard from Tim Tebow fell out.

A couple of years ago, Tim was in the news all the time. For his good manners and his clean living, but also because he would get down on his knees and say a prayer before every big game in front of a stadium of thousands—

probably millions, if you count those watching on TV. He wasn't your typical quarterback. And I liked that about him.

I liked him more when I heard what he said about having dyslexia. "There's a lot of people that have certain processing disabilities and it has nothing to do with intelligence."

I turned the postcard over. Standard size, full color. I'm sure he'd printed thousands. The front featured a picture of Tim and a quote from the Bible. "And now these three remain: Faith, Hope and Love. But the greatest of these is love."

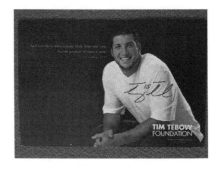

I wish he'd written something personal, but I can't blame him. I'm sure he gets thousands, maybe hundreds of thousands, of letters. At least he'd sent something.

On the back, he said, "Hard work beats talent when talent doesn't work hard."

There it was again. Hard work.

I'd read that Tim works very hard. He's always last off the field and first on. He can't memorize the plays from the playbooks like other football players—by watching them on-screen. He has to do the plays and then afterwards, he draws them onto index cards. He makes flipbooks with pictures that he goes through over and over and over and over.

I nodded. Not too different from what I do for tests. Over-learn.

One of Tim's coaches, Rex Ryan, is also dyslexic. He said, "When you look at it, it might not be the traditional way, but Tim finds a way to win."

Tim's an improviser, just like Thomas Sayre.

I want to win.

Can I win?

Tim Tebow'd probably say, "*How* can I (win)?"

When we got home, I tacked Tebow's postcard up next to Dr. Cosgrove and Thomas' letters. I added the letters from Princess Beatrice and Diane Swonk and even Ted Turner. The board was filling up. If I got any more, I'd have to take the poster down.

I went back to the question Tim might ask. *How* can I win?

It was clear I wasn't ever going to "win" on standardized tests or report cards.

Henry Winkler had asked, "What are your strengths?"

I didn't have an answer for that. Yet.

I saw *The Wiz* last night. It's a remake of *The Wizard of Oz*. Do you remember? With Dorothy, the Tin Man, the Lion and the Scarecrow... They follow the yellow brick road and run into screaming monkeys and witches and you think they're not going to make it to where they're going, but they finally do. They finally make it to Emerald City to see Oz. He's supposed to be able to give them the things they think they need. Do you remember now? The Lion wants courage and the Tin Man wants a heart... so, they go up to Oz and they ask him for courage and a heart and brains and a trip back to Kansas. Do you know what Oz says? He says, "I'm sorry. No can do."

And they're like "what do you mean?"

And he says, "I don't have any magical powers."

"What?" they say incredulously.

And you know what Oz says? He says, "Don't you see? You already have everything you need..."

They look around confused.

"...right inside you."

Thomas Sayre, Henry Winkler, Tim Tebow... they

didn't start out like other kids in school, confident that they had something special inside them. But, somehow, just like Dorothy and the Tin Man, in getting down and just doing the work, they found out that they did.

I listened to the Mexican workers across the street yelling commands. "Arriba, arriba! Cuidado!" I looked out the window. Someone was pulling a window frame up to the third floor using a rope and pulley system.

I looked at the letters tacked up in front of me.

They were really starting to add up.

When I started this, I didn't have any faith that they would, but here I was, just continuing to put one foot in front of the other. I still didn't know where it was all going to lead, but maybe that was okay.

Hard work beats talent
when talent doesn't work hard.
— Tim Tebow

13 IT TAKES THE TIME IT TAKES

"Drop your pants. Cough. Breathe. Don't blink. This isn't going to hurt at all."

It was time for my annual physical.

"Anything you want to talk about?" Dr. Burleson asked.

She rolled her stool over to her laptop on the desk and entered some numbers. "Any changes at home?" she asked while continuing to type.

"Pop's getting sicker," I said.

"Your dad?" she asked.

"No. Granddad."

"He lives with you?"

I nodded.

"I'm sorry," she said, typing in something. "That must be hard."

"Yeah," I said. "Dr. Burleson, am I ever going to grow?" I asked.

She was quiet as she scrolled through several more screens.

"All of my friends are shaving..."

She looked up. "When did Aidan's dad hit puberty?" she asked Mom.

"Seventeen. Eighteen?" Mom answered, without looking up from her magazine.

"And you?" she asked my mom.

"Maybe seventeen," Mom said.

"Another year, Aidan," Dr. Burleson said cheerfully. "Maybe two."

I groaned.

"You know what that means," she said.

I knew too well. No dates. No prom. No girls — except

those wanting to talk to me about going to the prom with other boys.

Dr. Burleson interrupted, "It means after all your friends stop growing, you're going to keep growing. On into college."

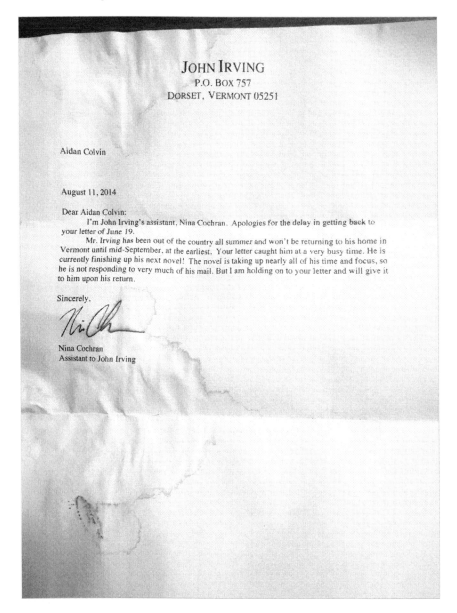

JOHN IRVING
P.O. BOX 757
DORSET, VERMONT 05251

Aidan Colvin

August 11, 2014

Dear Aidan Colvin:

I'm John Irving's assistant, Nina Cochran. Apologies for the delay in getting back to your letter of June 19.

Mr. Irving has been out of the country all summer and won't be returning to his home in Vermont until mid-September, at the earliest. Your letter caught him at a very busy time. He is currently finishing up his next novel! The novel is taking up nearly all of his time and focus, so he is not responding to very much of his mail. But I am holding on to your letter and will give it to him upon his return.

Sincerely,

Nina Cochran
Assistant to John Irving

I raised my eyebrows.

Dr. Burleson shrugged and lifted her hands, "There are some things we can't control."

Yep, I thought. Like Pop's cancer and this project.

I thought I'd be finished by now. I'd sent out 100 letters. 100. Some repeats. (Jay Leno.)

I know people are busy and stuff. What did I expect? Truthfully, I didn't expect anyone to answer.

So when John Irving's assistant, Nina, wrote yesterday that she'd give him my letter in September, I got really excited. Really excited. And impatient. And hopeful. And frustrated.

I do that. I thought back to second grade when I was first diagnosed with dyslexia. I started going to a reading tutor. I thought I would just learn to read. Couple of weeks and I'd be back on track. It took over three years. Eight years later, I'm still a slow reader.

"No magic bullet," Mom said.

No magic bullet is right. God knows we tried to find one.

While looking, I came across this guy, Ben Foss, an inventor and a writer. He wrote a book called *The Dyslexic Empowerment Plan*. It's a little dense for a kid, but parts of it were useful. So I wrote to him. I told him I read his book. I told him about my project.

MAGIC BULLETS THAT DIDN'T WORK

- *Colored overlays*
- *Franklin Speller (reads words aloud, only works if you spell word correctly)*
- *Dragon Dictate on the PC—it didn't understand kids' voices)*
- *The Reading Pen (run it over a word and it reads it. Didn't work)*
- *A million apps and computer games*
- *Four leaf clovers, lucky pennies, rabbits feet, certain stuffed animals...*

I told him I was looking for heroes. I asked him if he had had a hero when he was my age.

You know what? He emailed me back. The day he got my letter!

He said General Patton was one of his heroes. Patton went to West Point, one of the best military colleges in the United States. He struggled. He was at the bottom of his class. But he stayed and focused on developing his strengths—which were strategic thinking, people skills, and verbal skills—and he ended up becoming one of the greatest field commanders in US history.

In his book, Foss shared a letter Patton sent to his dad when he was a freshman:

> I am nearly hopeless. I don't know what is the matter for I certainly work. I hate to be so low-ranking for I still think I am smarter than other men who outrank me... It is exasperating to see a lot of fools who don't care beat you out when you work so hard. I can't think of anything but my own worthlessness so I will stop writing.
>
> —Your goaty son

I can totally relate. It made me remember Dr. Cosgrove's story about applying to 13 medical schools and getting into only one.

In his email, Mr. Foss said that dyslexics get used to failing a lot early on. We sure do! Mr. Foss said that, because of this, dyslexics aren't as afraid to try new things.

He said that might help explain why 35% of American entrepreneurs—an entrepreneur is someone who dreams up and starts and runs their own company—are dyslexic.

You've probably heard of some of these dyslexic entrepreneurs or their companies: Henry Ford, Ingvar Kamprad... he founded Ikea. Richard Branson, President of Virgin Atlantic. Paul Orfalea, Founder of Kinkos. Anita Roddick, Founder of The Body Shop...

Ben Foss says several reasons why dyslexics are more likely to start or run their own company is that they're not afraid to fail and they tend to have good people skills. I know I've had to develop those because I often

Date:7.16.14

Name: Ben Foss

Profession: Author and Entrepreneur

Who was your hero as a kid and why?

When I was a kid I tried to hide my dyslexia. But I secretly liked Gen. George Patton. He is dyslexic and thought he was a failure when he was in school. It took him five years to get through West Point, finishing 139th in his class at the end of his first year. Yet he went on to be the greatest field commander of the US military in the 20th century and potentially ever. He used his dyslexic strengths: strategic thinking, strong interpersonal and verbal skills, and kinesthetic skills to be a great leader. I respect him for meeting challenges head-on and playing to his strengths.

Many dyslexics don't succeed, but you did. Can you point to someone or something that helped you become the success you are?

I'm not sure it's true that many dyslexics do not succeed. All of us face major challenges. And we all succeed in our own ways. If you measure success by entrepreneurship we end up being 35% of the entrepreneurs in the United States. That said we are also 41% of those in the prison population.

My mother and father were a great help to me when I was a kid. They loved me unconditionally and taught me how to stand up for myself. I also took tremendous solace when I met Joe Stutts. I even made a film about him. You can watch it here. He became the first dyslexic person to win a civil rights employment case in federal court and prove that dyslexia is a disability and that we are entitled to accommodations in the workplace. He did all this as someone with a sixth grade education still won a four-year legal battle against the government of United States. I respect him greatly and he is my personal hero.

Do you have a story from your life that might help me or others stay hopeful and keep trying when we've had a challenging setback because of the dyslexia?

My approach is always to focus on strengths. Figure out what you are good at and focus on them, not you weaknesses. There is a Ted talk I did about letting go of shame and playing to your strengths. I much prefer to tell you the stories with my voice than to write when possible. I do this in part because I know that many dyslexics are anxious about using text with their standard reading skills. I use text-to-speech engines in order to listen to tax at a very fast rate you can learn more about that here. This allows me to play to his strengths (strong auditory skill) and compensate for weakness (decoding text with my eyes)

What one piece of advice or wisdom would you give to a dyslexic kid today?

You are not broken. More often than not the educational system or the workplace you are in is broken, meaning it was not designed for people who are dyslexic or have other so called Specific Learning Disabilities.

As you grow up you should be proud of being dyslexic. It is a part of you just as being from your hometown is part of you.

Over time you should learn how to tell your story. A great way to do that is to learn more about dyslexia and www.headstrongnation.org. Above all, play your strengths. In the long term you'll be measured more by what you can do that by what you can't. Shame is your greatest enemy and you should practice telling your story to other people and learning how to be proud of who you are.

May I contact you directly if I have an additional question? If so, will you give me a phone number or email I can use? (I will not share it with anyone.)

My schedule is quite full. If you have follow-up questions please email me. Feel free to share the links about in any way you can. Good luck with the project!

Thank you!

have to ask friends for help or to share their class notes with me.

In his email, Mr. Foss said, "In the long-term, you'll be measured more by what you *can* do than what you can't." He told me to concentrate on my strengths and to be proud of who I was.

He also said—and this got my attention—I needed to learn how to tell my story. And how to be proud of it.

How to tell my story?

I thought about that for a minute.

When I'm in a good frame of mind, I joke about my dyslexia. For instance, last time I went to Dr. Burleson and filled out a survey about my health, I accidentally checked boxes to indicate that yes, I used marijuana, smoked cigarettes, drank alcohol and might be pregnant. Now I ask you... If that were true, why would I tell my doctor? I was mortified when she brought them up. What do you do? You learn to laugh it off.

But when I'm in a bad place, I lose faith that I'll ever graduate or get a job. I convince myself that I'll become one of those people who live in their parent's basement. Sometimes I can be my own worst enemy. Maybe there's something to what Mr. Foss said? Maybe I do need to figure out how to tell my story. And maybe I need to make that a better story.

Shame is your greatest enemy and you should practice telling your story and learning how to be proud of who you are. — Ben Foss

14 A NEW SCHOOL

School started this week. My schedule: Math II, Chemistry, Engineering, English and Study Hall.

I'm coming in as a tenth grader. Everyone already has friends. Except me.

When the lunch bell rang, I went back to the covered patio where everyone was eating. I looked around. I had no one to sit with. I walked around, watched some kids play football. I checked my phone. I went back in the building to go to the bathroom. I stayed for awhile. When I came back out, I pretended to be interested in the posters in the hall. Killing time, really. The bell finally rang. Chemistry. I hate chemistry.

"How was your first day?" Mom asked when she pulled up.

"No one talked to me," I slumped into the front seat. "The whole day."

"You want to drive?" she asked.

"Do you want to die?" I had just gotten my permit.

"You've got to practice," she offered.

"Not today," I said and slumped down into the seat.

She said, "This isn't the first time you're the new kid..."

I changed the subject. "What'd you do today?"

"I took Pop to radiation and then we went to get Polish Dogs at Costco," she said.

"That was nice," I said.

"Sherri picked him up this afternoon. He wanted to go home for a few weeks," mom said.

We both stared out the window. School. Pop's cancer—both unsolvable problems.

When we pulled into our driveway, I got out, grabbed

the mail and headed inside. I dropped my backpack and leafed through the stack.

Bill, bill, bill. I put those in Mom's stack. Backpacker Magazine. I put that in Dad's. Pop had gotten a few Get Well cards. I tossed the flyers and catalogues into the recycling bin.

At the bottom of the pile was a letter. To me?

I hadn't received a letter in almost a month. I put the project aside when school started. I wasn't quite sure what to do with it. And I didn't have the brain space to figure it out.

I looked at the envelope. It was from Vermont. I'd only written one person there. I carefully pulled the single sheet out. It was from John Irving. THE WRITER John Irving.

Have you seen *The World According to Garp*? That John Irving.

He wrote in a blue felt tip pen. He mentioned Charles Dickens as his hero. I hadn't read any Dickens. Well, we watched *A Christmas Carol* every year. We have some Dickens in English this year.

Irving said Dickens' stories were "both funny and sad."

I'd written Mr. Irving because I'd heard him in an interview on the radio. He'd said that he always started a book with the last line in mind.

I didn't start this book that way. Well, at one point I did imagine a final scene involving me and Jay Leno. Matching tuxes, bow ties. My braces would be off by then. Surely. Maybe I'd even finally have that growth spurt Dr. Burleson promised?

Date:

Name: JOHN IRVING

Profession: Novelist; screenwriter

Who was your hero as a kid and why? Charles Dickens, because his stories were both funny and sad.

Many dyslexics don't succeed, but you did. Can you point to someone or something that helped you become the success you are? School was hard; school is multi-tasking. I discovered that I was good at doing one thing, not many things. Writing a novel is one very long thing.

Do you have a story from your life that might help me or others stay hopeful and keep trying when we've had a challenging setback because of the dyslexia? You need to give yourself more time; it takes you longer to do things than it takes your friends. So what? If one do it well.

What one piece of advice or wisdom would you give to a dyslexic kid today? ↑ Same as above!

May I contact you directly if I have an additional question? If so, will you give me a phone number or email I can use? (I will not share it with anyone.) No. It takes me longer to do my thing, remember? I always need more time.

Thank you!

At this point, I know that ending is just too far-fetched.

I looked back at Mr. Irving's letter.

He said school was hard because it was multi-tasking. He said he was good at doing one thing at a time.

Ha! Me, too.

He also said he was slow.

Bingo.

But then he said something I didn't expect. He said, "So what if it takes you longer—if you do it well?"

I hadn't thought of it that way. I'd always thought slow equals bad, right? I googled Irving and clicked on his Wikipedia page. I wondered how long it took Irving to learn to write well. I read his page. It said that his first three books didn't get any recognition. It wasn't until his fourth, The World According to Garp, when he was 36, that he began earning a living as a writer.

He's 74 now. He's written 14 books. It takes him two to three years to write a book.

Two to three years.

So what if it takes you longer if you do it well?

I thought about that today.

My parents and I met with Mr. Schwenker, the principal at my new school, and my teachers. I was having a hard time keeping up. Mr. Schwenker suggested I consider taking a lighter load. He said he thought I was capable of taking the Honors level classes, but perhaps I should take one class less each semester and graduate one year later.

I protested.

Mr. Schwenker said, "Just think about it."

I thought about Mr. Irving's advice.

Maybe Mr. Schwenker was right?

The next day, I told my guidance counselor that I wanted to follow Mr. Schwenker's advice. For second semester, I decided to take one less class per semester and spend that extra period in curriculum assistance, where I could get one-on-one help from Ms. Heilman. I'll graduate a little later than my friends, but that's okay.

Mr. Irving also said that the extent of work he had to do in order to simply pass and graduate was perfect training for what he was doing now... writing and writing and writing and writing and finishing and publishing book after book after book.

Even though it takes him longer than other writers, he keeps producing bestseller after bestseller.

What is one extra year of high school in the great scheme of life?

John Irving would say, "So what? If you do it well."

> You need to give yourself more time. It takes you longer to do things than it takes your friends. So what? If you do it well.
> — John Irving

15 JACK

I got two **RETURN TO SENDERS** today. TWO. Tommy Hilfiger—a clothes designer up in New York. And Richard Branson. You know. President of Virgin Airlines. The billionaire.

I was disappointed. But, you know what? I wasn't as disappointed as I was after the first **RETURN TO SENDER**. Remember? Ozzy Osbourne.

I looked at the two envelopes and then put them in the back of my drawer. I felt a little tougher this time. I didn't take it so personally. It was just part of the process.

I guess that's partly because something that was a bigger deal happened last night. I went back to Exploris—my old middle school. My sister had orientation. I wanted to say hi to all my teachers. Helene, Meredith, Shannon, Vishali...

While I was talking to Vishali, this mom came up and introduced herself and said her son wanted to talk to me. Really? I thought she had mistaken me for someone else. I looked around.

"Sure," I said.

She nudged her son forward. He looked uncomfortably down at his shoes.

"This is Jack," his mom said. "He's going to be in Livia's class."

"Hi," I waved. "I'm Aidan."

Jack looked around the room at everyone but me.

His mom said, "We heard you have dyslexia." She paused, "So does Jack."

Jack looked pained. I knew that expression.

"Mom!" he said.

"Well, I'll let you talk," his mom said. Then she disappeared.

"My mom does stuff like that all the time," I told him. "Any questions?"

Jack shuffled his feet for a second, then said, "I heard there's a lot of homework."

"True," I nodded, then I added, "but it's manageable."

He looked like he didn't believe me.

"Really," I said. I had come from the same elementary school as him.

He looked down at his shoes.

I continued, "And the teachers here... well, they're really nice. They want you to do your best," I said. I had come to this school, steeled to endure another place where I just didn't measure up. But it wasn't like that at all. It was here that I first started thinking of myself as someone who wanted to learn, as someone who could learn.

"Do you have a laptop?" I asked.

"Not yet."

"Get an Apple," I said. "You can dictate your papers."

He looked puzzled.

"You say your paper aloud and your computer writes it down," I explained.

"Really?" he said.

"Yeah... It can also read it back to you."

Jack looked excited.

"What else?" I was talking aloud to myself. "Oh, yeah, I opted out of a foreign language in middle school. I could use that time for homework..."

"Really?"

I nodded. As I talked to him, I realized I'd already been doing what Thomas Sayre said dyslexics do well. Improvising.

I went on. "If I can't spell English words, what's

the point of spending all my brain power trying to spell Spanish ones?"

"Yeah," he nodded.

"Also," I added, "they have math help on Thursdays after school."

He looked like he wasn't interested.

I said, "A lot of people go. You don't have to feel embarrassed."

I saw his shoulders visibly relax.

"Plus," I added, "The teachers are more flexible. Like for one project, instead of doing a paper, I made a movie."

"A movie?" he asked.

"It's easy on the Mac."

I suddenly remembered myself starting sixth grade here, looking and feeling very much like Jack did now.

"Do you have an IEP?" I asked directly.

He blushed.

"That's a good thing," I said. "Then you can get accommodations during tests... like extra time or a quiet place to take it..."

He seemed to consider that.

I smiled.

He smiled back.

I added, "you're going to be fine." And I believed it.

"Thanks," he said, adding, "Really." He put his hands in his pockets and nervously looked around the room. He caught his mom's eye and nodded.

Before she walked up, he said, "Thanks again."

"Done?" his mom asked.

We both nodded.

"See ya," he said to me.

"Yeah, later," I said, waving. "Call... if you need anything," I added.

He and his mom smiled and waved goodbye.

I waved back.

And they walked off.

I watched them. It suddenly occurred to me that I used to be Jack. That that used to be me.

Used to be.

Only four years ago. I'd come a long way since then.

I still have a ways to go. In high school, and college, and if I'm lucky, a job.

But it felt good to tell Jack he was going to be all right. And I wasn't joking. I really thought he would be.

I wonder if the people who've written me back think that about me?

16 STORMS

It's hurricane season in North Carolina and we've had a lot of rain. Mom and Dad were in the basement last night, trying to plug up holes in the mortar. The water was pouring in, almost like a faucet. Mom positioned large plastic bins along the walls where the leaks were biggest. It's the downside of living in an old house.

My sisters spent all day today cleaning it up. They wanted to have a place where they could do gymnastics. I helped. We threw out some old costumes and boxes of stuff damaged by the rain.

After dinner, Liv and Sarah said, "Come see what we did." And Mom and Dad and I went down there and I have to admit, it looked pretty good. We all sat down in some old blue chairs. Dad sat in Pop's old barber chair. (We got one, after he closed his shop.)

Livia said, "Well, what do you think?"

"Looks great," I said. I meant it.

Dad nodded, "Yeah."

The girls were bouncing up and down.

Mom smiled.

Dad cleared his throat. Then he said, "I've got something serious to tell you all."

Everyone got silent. Sarah went over to sit beside mom.

Dad paused and looked down. "Pop's cancer has come back."

It had come back three times now.

"We'll treat it again, right?" I said.

Mom put her arm around Sarah.

Dad said, "It means there aren't any other treatments."

I looked at the floor.

Dad added softly, "It means this time he will die."

Sarah burst into tears and hid her face in mom's sweatshirt.

"Sherri is bringing him here tomorrow," Dad said. "For radiation for his headaches."

Livia started blinking hard.

We all just sat there. Sarah sniffled. Livia got up jerkily and ran upstairs. We heard her feet pounding the steps up to her room. And then her door slammed.

"How long...?" I started.

"Not long," Dad answered quickly. "Maybe two, three months?" He let out a long sigh, then stood up and walked silently upstairs. I listened to his footsteps. Then I started to cry. Mom motioned for me to join her and Sarah. I shook my head and walked upstairs alone.

The first thing that came to mind when I got to my room was that I needed to finish this project. I wanted to give it to Pop. We were on a deadline. A true dead-line.

I sat down at my desk. I opened up my laptop. At the top of the screen was a message. "You've got mail." I scrolled through my email. There were some from school. Delete. Delete. Delete. Delete. Some from friends. Some junk mail. But then I came across the name Phillip Schultz. Phillip Schultz. That name sounded familiar.

Phillip Schultz, I said it to myself again. I opened the email.

Then I remembered. My mom's cousin Carolyn had sent me an essay Schultz had in the New York Times. It was from his book, *My Dyslexia*. He was a poet up in New York. After reading his essay, I wrote him. The letter had been returned to sender, but then I emailed it to a secretary at his writing school. I had forgotten about it. She must have forwarded my letter on to him. And he'd emailed me back. Awhile ago. I was embarrassed. I hadn't noticed it.

It was odd to read his email right after John Irving's letter. If reading and writing came so hard to both of them, how did either become a writer?

I read his letter.

He said his two heroes were the painter Vincent van Gogh and the writer Ernest Hemingway, artists who made him "feel and think deeply."

I sat back. Who were writers who made me feel and think deeply? Harper Lee certainly had in *To Kill A Mockingbird*. So had John Steinback in *Of Mice and Men*. Both books were hard to put down, tragic and stayed with you.

I hadn't read any Hemingway. But I would now.

I scrolled further down.

It was encouraging that he got into college even though he was a "bad student." I wondered what he meant by "bad."

I mean I'm a bad student. And what I mean is I'm making B's and C's and one D at this point. I have an A in English. English! And I'm dyslexic.

I don't know if I'll get accepted to any college with those grades. Mom says there's a place for everybody. Livia added, "In your case, the women's correctional facility."

I read further. I stopped when I came to this sentence: "I see young people for whom things come very easily and although their lives are—I am quite sure—easier than mine, I feel that dyslexia gave me an advantage."

Here it is again. That idea that a hard experience can make you stronger. Even give you an advantage.

I was relieved to hear Mr. Schultz say that everything gets better after high school.

Right now, everything feels hard. Not just school. Knowing that we're going to lose Pop... that makes everything feel hard, too.

Hi Aidan,
Thank you for your patience in receiving the answers to your questions. Even long after you finish 9th grade, the end of the school year is a very busy time.

Name: Philip Schultz
Profession: Poet, Founder and Director of The Writers Studio

Heroes as a kid: Originally, I would say Vincent van Gogh. "Starry Night" inspired deep and powerful feelings in me long before I could understand why. I originally wanted to be a painter. When I finally began reading without too much pain, I discovered Ernest Hemingway, and then I knew I wanted to be a writer. I would say my heroes have always been creative artists who inspire me to feel and think deeply.

College questions: I originally went to University of Louisville, partly because it was far away from Rochester NY, where I grew up, and partly because they accepted me. I came from a very poor family and was not a good student in high school, so I felt lucky to go there. I then transferred to San Francisco State, where the writing program was very strong. I am still indebted to and involved with SF State, a school that prides itself on educating students who have backgrounds similar to mine. I became a poet there, and yes I did graduate. There were no tools available to help me with the logistics of schoolwork back then. I was a writer, so I read slowly and wrote longhand. I went on to earn an MFA from the Iowa Writers Workshop at the University of Iowa.

What helps explain my success: I think my dyslexia helped me focus on the things I can do and own up to the things I couldn't do (or do well). So I specialized in writing and teaching very early on. I see young people for whom things come very easily, and although their lives are -- I am quite sure -- easier than mine, I feel that dyslexia gave me an advantage. I also work very hard and put in a lot of hours.

Do I have a story to help others stay hopeful and persistent? Aidan, I wrote a memoir, "My Dyslexia," (published by WW Norton) which tells my whole story, and which many people have found quite heartening. I will tell you something I haven't told anyone else: The person who asked me to write that book had a dyslexic son exactly your age, and the purpose of the book was to give him hope and persistence.

Practical Advice: Use your foreign language exemption. It would have saved me a lot of strife in school if that had been available.
Life Advice: Keep finding delight in your word-play. Use your dyslexia as a tool to find your way. Everything gets better for dyslexics after high school.

Take Care, Aidan, and have a great summer.

Philip Schultz

I opened up my scrapbook. I pulled out a picture of me and Pop in his garage working on a lathe. I tacked it up on my bulletin board amid the letters, and then I lay down on my bed. I could hear Mom go into my parent's bedroom. I could hear Dad crying. I looked back at Mr. Schultz's letter. I scanned my bookshelf for a moment, then I saw what I was looking for: a book by Hemingway. I pulled it down. It was old and dusty. It hadn't been opened in a long time. I began to read it.

> Use your dyslexia as a tool to find your way.
> — Phillip Schultz

17 MY FIRST INTERVIEW

My mom pulled up to the carpool lane and I slid in. I waved goodbye to Kayla. She's Chinese and has long black hair. She smiled and waved back.

"Looks like you've made a friend," mom said.

"She's vice president of our class," I said. "She talks to everyone."

"Things take time," Mom said.

I grimaced. It had been two months.

Some guys started a game of pickup football during lunch. I stood on the sidelines and watched. No one asked if I wanted to play.

"How was your day?" I asked Mom.

"I took Pop to the doctor's and then to Side Street for lunch," she said. Side Street was a little restaurant in our neighborhood. Pop loved Mary Lu's pimento cheese.

"That was nice," I said.

"It made him happy," she said. "Your rowing clothes are in the back."

I climbed into the back seat to change before we picked up Julia and Charlotte.

"You excited?" Mom asked.

We had our first regatta coming up in High Point that weekend. Coach said I'd be coxing one or two boats. She didn't know which ones yet.

"Nervous," I said, while pulling on a t-shirt.
She pulled into the semicircle in front of St. Mary's. We had a few minutes to kill before the bell rang.

"No need to be," she said. "You're racing against other beginners."

All first-year high school aged rowers are novice until they have two seasons under their belt. Then they move to Varsity.

"I don't want to let my crew down," I said.

I climbed back into the front seat next to her and pulled on my shoes. I saw the first students leaving St. Mary's. A text message popped up on my phone.

I didn't recognize the number. Whoever it was introduced herself as Marritt, Harvey Hubbel's assistant. She said Harvey had gotten my letter and wanted to schedule a Skype call. He was available this Friday. My heart started beating fast. I turned to Mom.

"Are we doing anything on Friday?" I asked.

"I don't think so. Why?" she said.

"Because I need to call Harvey."

"Harvey?"

"The filmmaker."

She didn't say anything.

"You know, the one who just finished that documentary on dyslexia."

"Oh," she said, looking down at her calendar. "You've got rowing."

I said, "I've got to do this interview."

I dictated a response to Marritt. "That would be great. What time?"

She texted back immediately. "How about 3?"

I dictated, "Great. Is there anyway we could see a rough cut of *Dislecksia: The Movie* beforehand?"

"Sure," she texted back. "I'll send a link and password."

"Thanks," I dictated. "I'll call you at 3 pm."

Mom said, "Here they come."

Julia slid into the back seat. Charlotte was right behind her.

"Hey guys. How was your day?" Mom asked, looking in the rearview mirror.

"Great," Julia said.

"Hope you're ready," Charlotte said, ominously,

"Coach is going to have everyone erg a 5k today."
Erging is rowing on one of the rowing machines.

"We're not out on the lake?" I asked. It was beautiful out.

"No, he wants to see everyone's times," said Charlotte, "so he can set the lineups for High Point."

"Oh," Julia looked panicked. She was novice, like me.

"Are we doing anything important Friday?" I asked.

"Loading the boats..." said Charlotte.

"I've got something," I said, "important."

"Coach Will won't let you miss when you're Varsity," Charlotte warned.

I nodded.

. . .

The week dragged by.

I set up a Skype account. On Friday, I put my phone on a small tripod to film the call.

At 2 on the dot, my computer started to ring. A young, good-looking brunette flashed onto the screen. I heard a man's voice.

"Do I look like Harvey?" it said.

I laughed nervously. Then the camera shook as someone passed the laptop over to a man with thick grey hair.

"Got ya," he laughed. "That was my assistant Marritt." He adjusted the tilt and position of his monitor.

"Alright, we're going to make a kid happy today," he said.

I gave him two thumbs up.

"Okay, go ahead, kid."

I was nervous. "I watched your documentary," I said. "It was amazing."

"Thanks," he said.

I asked him how he got the idea for it.

"Great question," he said, looking out into his production room while composing an answer. "I'm dyslexic. I wanted to raise awareness," he said. "But just 'cause I'm dyslexic doesn't mean I know that much about dyslexia, so I started reaching out to neuroscientists..." I looked at my phone to see if it was still recording. It was.

"...But..." he said, "a film full of just neuroscientists talking is not fun. Right?"

We both laughed.

"So then I started thinking of these really cool visual

PLAY THE TRAILER!

shots..." he went on. "All these scientists walking down a street, kind of like Reservoir Dogs. That could be cool..." he paused, "but that doesn't sell a film either. I've got to somehow explain what happened in the schools..." He went on to explain how he came up with the structure and contents of the film and found archival footage from old educational films that he could use in the movie to evoke the period when he was in school.

"Harvey," I interrupted. "Did you always know you wanted to be a filmmaker?"

"In high school," he said, "I wanted to be a writer, but people just laughed. They said, 'you're going to be a writer? You can't even spell.'"

Then he added, "But if you have a passion for something, if you want it bad enough, you're going to do it."

"Cool," I said. Then I asked, "How did you go from graduating from high school where you didn't even know how to write a resume to becoming a world renowned filmmaker who has won, like, three Emmys?"

"Four," he corrected, "but who's counting?" We both laughed again.

He went on, "When I was a kid, people figured dyslexics saw things backwards. That was the best people could make sense of dyslexia. Now we know it's just a difference in processing."

Harvey was quiet.

"Do you have any dyslexic stories from, um, your life?" I asked.

He paused.

"Yeah," he said. "I was in a little town called LA and I was shooting something and I was getting ready to fly back. This is after 9/11 and I go to get in line and I open up my wallet and I look to where my license is supposed to be and... there's no license."

He went on, "Now you gotta have a license to get on an airplane. Otherwise they think you're a terrorist. I was looking all over the place. I told my coordinator 'You take the master tapes and go,' and she said, 'no, I'm not going to leave you.' They were beginning to separate us..."

"Then this TSA agent says, 'where do you live? And I say 'Hutchinson Parkway.' And he says, 'how do you spell it?' And I say, 'I don't know how to spell. I'm dyslexic.' And the guy leans in to me and says, 'we're going to do this, man. Because my brother was dyslexic.'"

"And I knew right then that I was going to fly."

I got chills for a second.

He said, "I can't spell the road that I live on and that may really upset a first or a third grade teacher. They might say, 'come on Harvey, you're not trying hard enough.'"

"When you're young, you need an adult to advocate for you," he paused again, "but later you need to learn how to say to the teacher yourself, 'listen, I just don't learn that way. This is how I do it.'"

He went on, "We're not all going to do well on math or reading or standardized tests. We have different strengths. But you're not going to hire me to be your accountant. You're going to hire me to be your filmmaker."

There was silence.

"Um..." I wondered whether I could ask him this. "How did you get stars in your movie... like Billy Bob Thornton?"

He didn't miss a beat. "Kid, I'll tell you. You got to follow the rules. You got to get the addresses and information where you go through agents."

Agents? I thought. What's an agent? I didn't send any of my letters to famous people to their agents first.

He went on, "Agents want 10%. We're a documentary company. We're hardly scraping through with the costs of our overhead... But you ask, you ask, you ask. You re-ask. They tell you to call back. Eventually what happened is someone who knew someone called us back. With Billy Bob Thornton, he was going to give us an hour to set up and an hour to interview. With a celebrity like him, their agent came in at the beginning and said, 'Hey, you know you've got that phone call in an hour.' That's code for 'hey, if I don't want to hang out with you guys, I'm out of here in an hour.'

"So, after an hour, his coordinator came in and said, 'ok, you've got that phone call' and he said, 'no, man. I'm cool' and after the interview, we went off and shot some pool and wandered around."

"It's always a little different. With Billy Banks, I just kept running into him. I still hang out with him because he had really bad experiences as a kid and... Aidan?"

"Yeah?" I said.

"With us dyslexics, it's a community... We look out for one another."

I thought to myself, he's right. That's why I talked to Jack. Maybe that's why people have written back to me?

"Thank you so much, Harvey!" I said.

"No problem, kid. Now, you have time for a tour of my studio?"

"Yeah!" I said.

"Great," he said and he walked around the room with his laptop introducing me to everyone in the office and showing me his desk and his stuff and the stuff on his walls. It was the most awesome thing ever.

And it was something I never could have imagined when I started this project. But then, one thing led to another. And before too long, here I was, talking to an Emmy-Award-winning filmmaker like it wasn't such a big deal. But it was a big deal. It is a big deal. I mean, for the first time, I was starting to see myself as someone who might do something that's a big deal one day, too. Who knows how my story is going to end?

> *With us dyslexics, it's a community...*
> *We look out for one another.   — Harvey Hubbell*

18 MY FIRST REGATTA

Mom and I got up at 4:30 am. High Point was an hour and a half away and I needed to weigh in at 7 am. It occurred to me that this was the first sport where my size worked in my favor.

It was cold and grey and supposed to rain. We stopped at the Bojangles on New Bern Avenue for a biscuit, then pulled in next door for gas. Mom got out to pump. I turned on the audiobook we were listening to, *Boys in the Boat*. It's a true rowing story by Daniel James Brown about a group of underdogs from the University of Washington. It tells their long journey to the 1936 Olympics, where they took the gold medal.

Each chapter begins with a quote from George Pocock, one of the greatest boat builders ever. We were on Chapter Four. The narrator read,

> It is hard to make the boat go as fast as you want to. The enemy, of course, is the resistance of the water, as you have to displace the amount of water equal to the weight of men and equipment, but that very water is what supports you and that very enemy is your friend. So is life: the very problems you must overcome also support you and make you stronger in overcoming them.

Not so different from dyslexia.

I heard the pump click and Mom screw the cap back on. She slid in next to me. "What boats are you coxing?"

"Don't know yet," I said.

We pulled onto Capital Boulevard and then Wade Avenue and then I-40. It was still dark. Our high beams revealed a thick fog. I tucked my sweatshirt under my head and closed my eyes. It was going to be a long day.

Dad was driving the girls down to Wilmington today after Livia's gymnastics meet. It was Pop's 75th birthday. He had told everyone last week that he wanted a party. Not just to celebrate his birthday. To celebrate his life. He wanted to see everyone together for one last happy occasion.

So Aunt Sherri and Uncle Gary were cleaning his house. Uncle Bryan was driving down from Asheville with Aunt Hill to prepare a big shrimp boil.

Mom and I would get in late tonight after driving back to Raleigh to pick up the dogs. The party would start tomorrow after church.

I must have dozed off because when I opened my eyes next, we were pulling into a large grassy parking lot. Hundreds of cars were already there. Julia's family pulled their navy SUV in next to us.

Julia and I jumped out, grabbed our duffels and ran off to look for our team. We saw the trailer near one of the food shelters. Coaches White, Schaffer and Giles were already there, shouting commands. We had two Varsity fours going out. (That's four experienced rowers rowing with a coxswain.)

"Aidan," Coach Schaffer said, "I got you coxing three novice boats."

Three? I was terrified.

"Yeah, the boys and girls' novice eights and a mixed four," she said. "You're going to have to hoof it between the first two. The schedule's tight."

"Aidan!" Michael King gave me a fist bump. "You're coxing our mixed four, with Jack and Julia!"

Julia grabbed my shoulders in excitement.

"Aidan," Coach Schaffer said, "grab the other coxes and meet me down at the launch. We need to weigh in and look at the course."

I ran off to find Emma, Alexa, Sofie and Lauren. And

we ran down to the water where Coach White and Coach Schaffer were talking with the officials.

Coach said the course was tricky. While it was out and back, there was a tight turn at the orange buoy, which was just beyond the horizon. Buoys marked both sides of the river where it was too shallow to paddle. The wind was really picking up The High Point team had a definite advantage. They did all their training there.

Our varsity fours went out first. I yelled "Good luck" to Charlotte. It was starting to drizzle. I put a sweatshirt on and went down to watch. The boats were swinging wide. Charlotte's boat was favored to win and I saw that they had had a strong start. We yelled, "T-R-C! T-R-C! T-R-C!" (That's for "Triangle Rowing Club.") Then they dropped out of sight beyond the horizon.

When they reappeared, we saw that High Point had somehow passed them. What happened?

When they pulled in, they were fuming. High Point had cut them off at the buoy.

Coach Schaffer turned to me and said, "Aidan, it's the cox who loses or wins a race like this. You get to that buoy first and take it tight and you have a chance."

I pulled my crew together to tell them the plan. "Four power twenties, two power tens and we'll have extreme pressure on the port side when we hit the buoy," I said.

The drizzle turned to rain. The crew carried the boat down to the water. I pulled on my headset and climbed in. I barked, "Starboards to oar. Ports to oarlocks."

I looked over at Michael Pryor. I said, "Bow seat check. Two and four seat row. Three seat add in in two. One. Two."

We glided up to the start line. The official announced "Triangle, ready at line?"

I nodded. The official yelled, "Ready? Row!"

I yelled, "Build by fives. Power twenty in two. Now!"

The rain was coming down harder. I was having a hard time gauging how tight our course was. "Power twenty," I yelled. We flew, the shoreline falling behind. All I could hear was the rain hitting the shell, the paddles hitting the water and my voice. We hit the turn just right and cut neatly around the buoy and began our return.

"Starboard pressure. Ports light," I yelled into the rain. "Stroke seat hold!"

As we approached the shore, I heard our teammates yelling, "T-R-C! T-R-C! T-R-C!" Coach Schaffer was running along with us on the shore.

We crossed the finish line strong. The boys fell back, gasping for air. We coasted. Then the referee directed us to the take-out point.

I was straining to hear the results. Coach ran up. "You won!" she shouted. "You won the gold!"

She lifted me out of the boat and dropped me on the land. The referee told us to keep moving. Our teammates were cheering on the sidelines. I put back on the headset and barked out the commands and we carried our boat back up to the trailer.

I was shaking I was so cold. Someone threw a sleeping bag over me.

It was an amazing day.

I coxed three races. All three won golds.

I remembered what Henry Winkler had said to me, "Find your strengths, Aidan. Then run with them."

It occurred to me that maybe, just maybe, I might have found one.

> ...the very problems you must overcome also support you and make you stronger in overcoming them.   – George Pocock

19 POP

We pulled into Pop's driveway in Wilmington around 10 pm. I wore the gold medals into the kitchen. The first thing Uncle Gary said, "Is that all? Your sister won four."

I said, "You must still be sore that I beat you in that half marathon, Gary."

I went into Pop's room to say hello. He was sleeping. He woke up when he heard me. "Hello, my grandson," he said.

"Hi, Pop," I sat down on his bed. "How's your day?"

"Just resting," he said. "Seems like that's all I'm doing."

"Are you excited about your party?" I said.

"Sure," he smiled. "I'm proud of you, grandson." He pointed at my medals.

"Thanks, Pop," I said. "I'm going to let you get some sleep."

"Love you," he said and turned over on his pillow.

When I got up the next morning, the sky was bright blue. Uncle Bryan had already started boiling the potatoes and corn on a burner set up in the driveway. He was going to throw in the sausage and shrimp at the last minute. Mom and Sherri were setting up tables and drinks. The girls were dancing under the tent with Uncle Gary to Mardi Gras music.

Oh, when the saints...
Oh, when the saints...
Oh, when the saints...
Come marching in...

Gary was spinning one off in one direction, then the other. They were laughing hysterically. The dogs were going nuts. Bryan put the lid on the pot and joined in. Mom videotaped it.

I went out onto the screened porch, where Pop was sitting in his rocking chair.

"This is just what I wanted," Pop said. "I don't want people coming here just to see me sick and feel sorry. I want them to have fun."

"Well, they sure are," I said. And they were.

Dad was watching the cornbread in the oven when the first relatives started pulling up. First, Sonny, Pop's older brother, and his wife Martha. Then their daughter, Ginger, and her husband and son, Pete and Michael. Then Pop's younger brother, Robert, and his wife, Suzanne, and their daughter and granddaughter. And then Andy and Rea. And Dot. Everyone walked in to talk to Pop on the porch. The music continued to play.

> And when the sun begins to shine,
> Oh, when the sun begins to shine,
> Oh, Lord, I want to be in that number...
> When the sun begins to shine.

And soon the shrimp were ready. Bryan piled huge mounds of shrimp, corn and sausage on our plates. We poured tall glasses of icy lemonade and root beer and sat under the shade of the tent and cleaned our plates and then loaded them back up.

Then it was time for Aunt Sherri to bring out Pop's birthday cake. We all squeezed onto the porch where he was sitting. The kids led the song.

> Happy Birthday to you,
> Happy Birthday to you,

You look like a monkey,
And you smell like one, too.

Pop smiled and leaned over to make a wish and blow out the candles. They all went out. Everyone clapped. And Sherri started cutting the cake when all the candles reignited.

"What?" Pop said. He blew them out again.

We all watched. "Cut the cake," Pop said. Sherri picked up the knife again and then all the candles reignited.

"Oh, brother," Pop said. "Aidan, come help me."

I blew. But they reignited again. At that point, Uncle Gary started laughing.

Sherri said, "Gary, you should be ashamed..."

"Playing a joke on a man on his death bed," Pop said.

"Sorry," he said.

Everyone started laughing.

. . .

Later that afternoon, after everyone had left, I went into Pop's room. I brought my laptop. I had a draft of what I'd written so far about this letter-writing project. I wanted to read it to him. He and I were both dyslexic, after all. More than anyone else in my family, he understood what it was like.

"Hey Pop," I said. "Can I read you something?"

He said, "Sure. Sit right here," and he patted the bed beside him.

I opened the file on my computer.

He smiled and lay back to listen.

I read the first chapter. I saw him laugh at the part about my mom going through all my stuff and then quietly look out the window when I mentioned what the two girls said about me when I returned to the regular school.

I paused. "What do you think so far, Pop?" I asked.

"You're a good writer, my grandson," he said.

"Thanks," I said.

I was quiet for a minute.

"But..." he cleared his throat.

"Yeah?" I looked up.

"Well, Aidan..."

"Yeah?" I said again.

"Dyslexia..." he paused.

"Yeah?" I said once more.

He started again, "It's just that from here where I sit now..."

I didn't say anything.

"It doesn't matter..." he said.

"What do you mean... it doesn't matter?" I said.

"I mean in the end—being dyslexic—it doesn't matter," he said.

I looked at him quizzically.

He continued, "What matters..." he stretched his

arms out to encompass me and the room and the whole house. "What matters," he said again, "is this... family, friends, being surrounded by people who love you."
I sat there.

"Aidan," he said, "you have everything you need..." He held up his arm limply and swept it around, "out there and in here." He placed his hand on my chest. Then he looked out the window. "Remember that," he said.

I smiled.

"I love you, my grandson," he said.

"I love you, too, Pop," I said.

"I'm pretty tired," he said and closed his eyes.

I put my hand on his and sat there on the bed until he fell asleep. Then I stood up and gave him a soft kiss on the forehead. It's kind of like *The Wizard of Oz*. Maybe Pop was right. Maybe I already did have everything I needed.

You have everything you need...
out there and in here.   — Pop

20 THE NINTH LETTER

The response came in a large cushioned brown envelope. Inside was a letter on expedition stationary and a poster folded into fourths. It was from arctic explorer Ann Bancroft. She was the first woman to travel over 1000 miles in deep snow across Canada's Northwest territories to reach the North Pole. Seven years later, she led the first all-female expedition to the South Pole on skis. And in 2001, Ann and her Norwegian friend Liv Arnesen became the first women to ski across Antarctica.

I carefully unfolded the poster on my bedroom floor. It was a picture of Ann, a tiny red dot against a vast landscape of snow and sky, walking across Antarctica. Along the sky, she had hand-written "Remember... it takes millions of small steps to get across Antarctica, but they accumulate and suddenly, you're there."

"Sorry it's taken me so long to write back!" she started.

Ann is the ninth person I've heard from. I've had it in my head since the beginning that I wanted to hear from ten, that the project would somehow be complete then. Her letter had come in December long after I'd stopped watching the mail.

"I can't read her cursive." I said to Mom when I looked at the letter. "Will you?"

She nodded.

I handed it to her.

She read, "You asked me what has made the difference in helping me succeed. First and foremost, my parents. My mom in finding ways to keep me reading — so I could keep dreaming of all I wanted to do in this wonderful big world."

Ms. Bancroft went on to mention a special teacher, the woods and a sense of humor.

I wondered how Ann and Liv Arneson prepared to cross Antarctica? I went online. I found an interview with her. She said that she and Liv cross-country skied

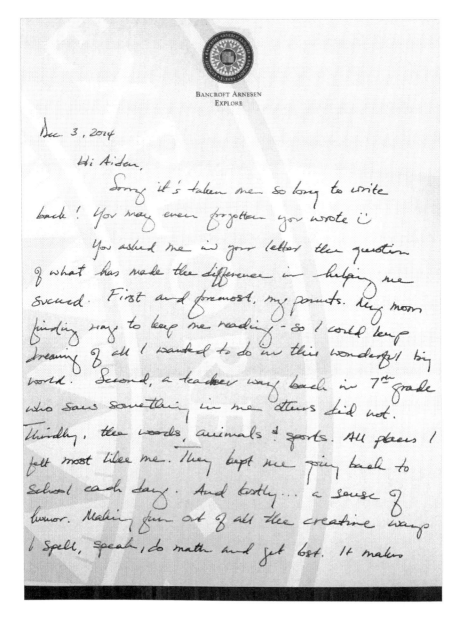

BANCROFT ARNESEN
EXPLORE

Dec. 3, 2014

Hi Aidan,

Sorry it's taken me so long to write back! You may even forgotten you wrote me

You asked me in your letter the question of what has made the difference in helping me succeed. First and foremost, my parents. My mom finding ways to keep me reading - so I could keep dreaming of all I wanted to do in this wonderful big world. Second, a teacher way back in 7th grade who saw something in me others did not. Thirdly, the woods, animals & sports. All places I felt most like me. They kept me going back to school each day. And lastly... a sense of humor. Making fun out of all the creative ways I spell, speak, do math and get lost. It makes on gravel roads while pulling three car tires harnessed to their waists. They ran up and down steep bluffs with 50-pound bags of kitty litter in their backpacks.

Ann said, "My dyslexia and my challenges through school were the absolute perfect training for an expedition. Expedition people are all about one step in front of the other and not going very fast, just doing the hard work." Remember what John Irving said? The extent of work he had to do in order to simply pass and graduate was perfect training for what he was doing now... writing and publishing books.

Ann said, "What better way to get the work ethic than by having a learning difference?"

Mom looked up from the letter. "Aidan, is this the end of the story?"

"It's the ninth person I've heard back from," I said, "but..."

"This might be it," she said.

"It's not the ending I—" I said.

"Guess what?" Mom interrupted me.

I looked up.

"I was swimming with Helen," she said, "and I mentioned your project."

"Mo-oom..."

Helen was one of my friend's moms. I didn't want my friends to know.

"Helen said she knows the guy who finds cars for Jay Leno..."

"And?" I said.

"What if you sent what you've got so far to Jay through Helen's friend?"

I sat back. It would mean waiting for a response. It could be another six months. Or longer. There were no guarantees. I looked at Mom. "It's worth a try..." I said. What's the worst that could happen?

Jay doesn't write back?
Big deal.
That's life.

• • •

So that's what I did.

I looked at my letter to Jay Leno one last time.
Along with it was a draft of what I'd written so far.
I had tentatively titled it, "Looking for Heroes."

Mom's friend Helen had spoken to her friend Steve,
and Steve had said he would give it to Jay next time he
saw him—though he didn't know when that would be.

I remembered what Harvey Hubbell had said about
contacting stars. I'd found the names and addresses of
Jay's agent and his publicist.

I would send this to them, too. I wanted to get
them all in the mail this afternoon. We were heading to
Pop's house for Christmas tomorrow. We usually hosted
Christmas, but he was too sick to leave home.

I looked at the three envelopes. They were thick.
They were heavy.

I remembered not too long ago sitting at my dining
room table stuffing envelopes with my sister Sarah.
This whole idea had seemed like such a long shot back
then. And look what
had happened. It was an
important lesson. I put
the three envelopes in
a basket by our mailbox.
Then I went inside. I
went upstairs to pack
for Christmas at Pop's.

• • •

The next day, when we arrived with the dogs and decorations and presents, I said, "We brought Christmas, Pop."

"You sure did," he said.

We chopped and cooked and stirred and blended Christmas Eve dishes and finally everyone sat down to a big meal together. We pushed Pop up to the head of the table in his favorite chair. Pop said the blessing. And then we ate. It was all of his favorite dishes: lima beans, turkey and gravy, homemade mashed potatoes, buttery rolls. Pop ate a little of each, then nodded off.

After the dishes were cleared, we wheeled him into the living room near the tree. We then divided into three teams of dancers for a mock "talent show." It was family against family.

Aunt Hill and Uncle Bryan dressed in black leotards. They had duck-taped glow sticks to the leotards, which they then flickered on and off while dancing in the dark to "Hello," by Adele.

Aunt Sherri and Uncle Gary swept through the room in bird costumes, torn from old curtains, while dancing to "Sail."

Livia, Sarah and I did an interpretive dance to "Hello."

It was pretty clear who won.

We laughed. All of us. Even Pop.

Then Mom gave everyone a "Top Banana" award.

Here is my last picture with Pop. It was taken right

before Mom, Liv, Sarah and I left for home. Uncle Bryan and I had put on Pop's caps. I sat beside him. I told him what a great Pop he had been. I tucked his blanket around his body. I told him I loved him. And then I kissed him for the last time. I kissed him goodbye.

Stay your course. Do your passions, but do it your way. Just put one foot in front of the other. You'll get there.
    — Ann Bancroft

21 ENDINGS

It poured the day before the funeral, sheets and sheets of rain. The sun finally came out, just as we drove up to the grassy knoll surrounded by live oaks where Pop would be buried. Uncle Bryan read a short essay by John Muir and Dad said a few words. Then Wyatt, one of Pop's former boy scouts, told this story.

Wyatt said, "Pop had been a scout leader for 18 years. He'd been a woodworker for forty." He held up a wooden bowl fashioned out of a rotten piece of wood. Wyatt said that this bowl was emblematic of Pop. The wood in this bowl came from a maple that was rotten and discolored, yet Pop had still seen promise in it. He had fashioned it into a beautiful bowl that highlighted the wood's flaws, rather than tried to hide them. Wyatt said that Pop had acted similarly in his role as a scout leader, encouraging especially those boys who were troubled or rejected.

After the funeral ended, we drove back to Pop's house. We closed the door to his bedroom and went into the kitchen. We laid out all the food that friends and neighbors and family had dropped off. The rest of the day relatives, neighbors, old customers and friends stopped by to tell us stories or give us a hug or bring more food. And then, several days later, we drove home.

• • •

On what was supposed to be our first day back to school, we had an ice storm and school was cancelled. A bunch of kids from the neighborhood came over. We spent the morning sledding down Pell and Boundary Streets. We had just come back to the house for lunch when the call came in.

From Beverly Hills. Dick Guttman, Jay Leno's publicist. It was 1:58 pm our time, 10:58 his.

Mom answered.

Mr. Guttman asked in a brusque New York accent, "Is this Aidan's mom?"

She ran downstairs and motioned for me to come up. I had just dropped my wet snow pants on the floor. I motioned for everyone to be quiet. Then I bounded up the stairs after her. We closed the door to my room so we could hear better.

Mom put Mr. Guttman on speaker phone. "I don't want to be rude,' he said, rudely, "but... I have to be honest with you. I've got seventy other requests for Jay Leno's time sitting on my desk from this month alone. Seventy!" he repeated. And then he repeated it again, for effect. "Seventy!"

I panicked. Was there another kid writing the same book as me?

Mr. Guttman continued, "I mean Jay gets approached all the time to make volunteer appearances for this or that group, or to do this or that. His schedule is tight. Really tight."

My mom looked over at me and said, "I see."

Mr. Guttman went on to say Jay makes several volunteer appearances a year for the military— he flies out to them, wherever they are. That's all he can fit in." He added that Leno was totally booked up now— especially with his upcoming new series, *Jay Leno's Garage*..."
Mom interrupted, "We understand, but..."

Mr. Guttman cut her off and said, "You're asking me to read the book and somehow endorse it and maybe publicize it...?"

"No," my mom said, "no, no, no. What about a five-minute interview? Just four questions...?"

"It'd be irresponsible for me to let him do that without reading the whole book..." Mr. Guttman said. "And I don't have time for that."

Mom appeared to be thinking. "I see," she said.

"I mean I assume it extols him..." he went on.

"Of course," Mom said. "That's why Aidan picked him."

Mr. Guttman paused, then said, "The one thing I've learned from Jay that sets him apart is he's humble. He genuinely is."

"We know," Mom agreed.

"But I'm still going to have to say no," Mr. Guttman said.

We were both silent for a moment.

"Thanks," I said. "Thanks for calling back."

"Goodbye then," Mr. Guttman said.

"Goodbye," we said.

He hung up. We looked at each other. Then we both looked down at the floor.

What did this mean?

"His publicist called..." Mom said. "From Beverly Hills!"

Harvey Hubbell had been right. I'd written Jay Leno directly three times without any answer, but I got a call from his publicist the day he received my letter and book. I guess I'd learned something about how things worked in show business.

Mom didn't say anything for a minute, then said, "What do you think?"

I stared down at the floor.

"This isn't the ending I imagined," I said, thinking out loud.

For the last year, I'd dreamed about coming onto stage at Jay's upcoming show in North Carolina and giving him a copy of my book. I had an outfit picked out:

a black velvet jacket I'd found at a flea market, a red bowtie, some cufflinks I got for Christmas...

Mom said, "...but it might be the ending you have to work with."

I looked down. I looked over at my desk. I looked at the letters pinned to the corkboard... Dr. Cosgrove. Princess Beatrice. Diane Swonk. Ann Bancroft. Ted Turner. Thomas Sayre. Phillip Schultz, Ben Foss, Tim Tebow...

All these people had taken the time to write me.

I stared at their letters.

Sure, they gave me some really great practical tips, but there was something else, something more important...

What?

I looked down at the floor.

Mom sat silently.

They let me know I wasn't alone.

They let me know, in fact, that I was standing with some pretty amazing company.

I looked at Mom. "I can work with this ending."

22 THE JAY LENO SHOW

It was Friday afternoon, when Mom pulled up to the school to pick me up early. We had tickets to see Jay Leno in Fayetteville. It was about an hour and a half's drive away. When we bought the tickets eons ago, the show had seemed so far off. But here we were.

"Excited?" Mom asked, when I slid in.

I had just gotten back a chemistry quiz. I got an F. And I had studied. A lot. I was frustrated.

"I'm sorry," Mom said, when I told her. "Let's worry about that tomorrow."

I stared out the window. Chemistry. It's all symbols that represent words I could never sound out or remember. And combined with math. I studied, attended study lunch, afterschool tutoring... I even watched additional videos. It didn't seem to matter. I was still drowning.

"We're going to have an early dinner with Kate and Aunt Sarah," Mom said.

Aunt Sarah was Pop's aunt, so I guess that made her my great, great aunt. She is smart and feisty and 92-years old. Every October her daughter Kate hosts a big barbecue celebration of Aunt Sarah and Pop's birthdays. This year, Pop's place at the table would be empty.

We pulled into their gravel driveway. Kate came out on the porch.

"Have you told him?" she asked my mom.

"What?" I asked.

Kate looked at me.

"Kate told me to write Bill Kirby," Mom said.

"He writes for the Fayetteville Observer," Kate added.

I looked at Mom.

"I told him your story..." Mom said.

"And?"

"He's going get you in to meet Jay before the show."

"What!" I said. "Really?"

Mom nodded. "Only for a quick photo. He doesn't have any time to talk."

I couldn't believe it.

"Come visit with Momma," Kate said, as she led us into the living room. "I'm going to go finish putting dinner out."

We sat down and talked with Aunt Sarah and Kate's husband, Pat. Then Kate spread a feast of cold cuts and fruit salad and homemade apple dumplings on the kitchen table. Her husband Pat asked me about fishing. Aunt Sarah asked about rowing. Kate kept passing me dishes. Finally, I pointed to the time.

Mom looked at it. "Oh, we should get going," she said, standing up. I stacked everyone's empty plates and carried them to the sink.

"You sure you don't want another apple dumpling?" Kate asked.

"I'm all set, thank you," I said.

Kate said she would drive over in front of us so we wouldn't get lost. I excused myself and went to the bathroom. I put on my black velvet blazer and red bow tie. I tucked my red handkerchief in my breast pocket. I slicked back my hair.

"Now, there's no guarantee you'll meet him," Kate said, "I don't want you to be disappointed if it doesn't happen."

"Look at you," Aunt Sarah said.

"So handsome," Kate added.

Mom said, "Let me get a picture of you all on the porch."

Then we got in the car and followed Kate out to the Coliseum.

We arrived thirty minutes before the doors opened. Kate showed us where to park and introduced us to Candice, someone from her church who worked the ticket booth. We waved goodbye, then mom and I sat in the car waiting for the coliseum doors to open. I was fidgeting. I had a copy of the book just in case. I was rolling the book up, then flattening it out. I was getting more and more nervous.

"What should I say?" I asked Mom.

"Just be yourself," she said.

Simple enough. It didn't help though.

And then the doors opened. We asked the man taking tickets where we could find Bill Kirby and he pointed us to a table over to the right where a small group of sponsors was gathering. We got in line. A helpful young lady with a clipboard asked for our email address and explained that everyone in line would get five seconds for a photo with Mr. Leno. She would email it to us. Then she disappeared with the first couple. We waited. It was finally our turn. She took us back.

There were nine people in this little area behind the stage. Jay Leno was casually standing in front of the Coliseum backdrop. A photographer was positioned in front of him. Three managers were to the side. The woman with the clipboard motioned for us to approach Jay. Mr. Kirby swept in.

He immediately asked, "Are you Aidan?"

"Yes, sir."

"Come right over here," he said and he led me over to Jay and introduced us. Jay said he was very glad to meet me and asked what I was holding.

I said I had spent the last year writing to dyslexic heroes, like him. I told him I had kept a diary of the process and made it into a book. I said I had written to him several times.

"Did I answer?" he asked.

"No," I smiled.

"I'm sorry. I get so many letters. I have so many people between me and the public and..."

"It's fine," I reassured him.

Then Jay went on to say that when he was a kid, they didn't know what dyslexia was. When he failed a test, his teachers would slap him on the side of the head and say, "smarten up."

I laughed.

"Now, at least," he said, "you can say, 'I'm dyslexic.'" Then he added, "just don't take any job where you have to write down hundreds of phone numbers and you'll be fine."

The woman handling the line pointed to her watch, but Jay went on. "Most dyslexics figure out what they like and go deep into it. They become really, really good at it. I have a friend who's a mechanical engineer and really successful and he's dyslexic."

Jay paused, then said, "And look at you. You've written a book. When I was your age, I wasn't even reading.

I smiled, "I brought a copy."

Jay took it and opened it up. He asked, "you took the initiative to write all these people?"

I nodded.

"That's great," he said. "What's your phone number?"

I scribbled it on the cover.

"Thanks," he said. "I'll call you when I'm done."

"Thanks!" I said. We turned to go.

Then Jay said, "Wait. Here. Take this. It's from The Tonight Show."

I caught the faded navy hat. "Really? Thanks so much!"

And then we were swept out to our seats.

"He asked for my phone number," I said.

"He's so busy..." Mom said.

"I don't expect him to call," I said quickly. "Mom, this was the best night of my life."

She smiled. And we hadn't even seen the show.

> Don't take a job taking down hundreds
> of phone numbers and you'll be fine.
> — Jay Leno

23 WELCOME TO THE REAL WORLD

We didn't get home until after midnight that night. And then the next morning, Julia and her mom pulled into our driveway at 5 am to pick us up for another regatta.

"I want to know everything," Julia said, when I slid into the backseat. I had posted the shot of Jay and me on Instagram.

"He was so down-to-earth," I said. I went on to tell her how Mr. Kirby had gotten us backstage and what Jay had said and then I told her some jokes from the show.

"You're so lucky," she said.

"I know," I said. "I know."

An hour and a half later, the car turned onto the gravel drive leading to Oak Hollow Lake. It was a gorgeous day, sunny and clear. Julia and I ran down to weigh in at the coxswain tent and then helped rig the boats.

I was assigned to cox the four-person boys' novice boat and the eight-person boat, too.

We got lucky. Both won golds--which means I was tossed in the lake. That's what happens to the coxswain if your boat takes first.

After de-rigging the boats and loading them onto the trailer, we piled back into Virginia's car and headed home. My friends decided to go out to dinner and a movie to celebrate. I was too tired. I'd only slept a couple of hours the night before.

Virginia dropped us off at home.

I waved goodbye to everyone. Mom glanced at her phone. "Oh, I need to call Dad. Looks like he's been trying to reach us."

She unlocked the front door, while holding the phone to her ear. Then she started speaking to him. She hung up.

"That's odd," she said. "He said he hasn't called. Who else with a blocked caller ID would call?"

I went up to my room and started straightening it up from the school week. I had just put on some music when Mom started banging on my door.

"Aidan! Aidan!" she said.

I unlocked the door. She was pointing to the phone.

I looked at her, puzzled.

"It's Jay Leno," she whispered.

Oh my God. Oh my God.

She said into the phone, "I'm going to put you on speaker phone, okay?"

She closed my door and laid the phone on the floor between us.

"Hey, Jay Leno here," a voice called out. "How're you doing?"

"Great!" I said.

We both leaned over the phone.

"Aidan, I read the whole book," he said, "and I thought it was terrific."

"Really?" I said. Was this really Jay Leno?

"Yeah," he said. "I wouldn't tell you that if I didn't mean it."

I didn't know what to say. "Thanks," I finally managed. Then I asked, "Do you have any advice?"

He said, "Have you given a talk about it? Go give a talk. Answer questions. Bring the tape recorder. Listen to it afterwards. Say you got asked fifty questions and ten were really good and so you put ten really good answers into your next talk—and your book."

He continued, "That's what I tell actors to do. When they don't have a movie, go to a college and ask to speak. And they say, 'I don't know how to speak.' But they do it and then what happens is they find out they have all these funny stories and advice inside of them and it comes out."

"That's a great idea," I said.

"Yeah," he said, "I'd also go to the English department of whatever university is close and ask a teacher to give you a scathing review. Everything needs editing, no matter who you are. How do you make your story really great?"

He went on, "when I write a joke, I drive around in the car and practice it in my head. I say it to myself over and over and over until I get rid of all the little parts that really aren't funny. Just get it down to its basics."

Oh my gosh, I thought to myself. I think he's telling me how Jay Leno became Jay Leno.

Then he said, "You know the Smothers Brothers? They were a folk singing duo. The interesting thing is that Tommy had dyslexia. So Tommy would get the words wrong and people would laugh, and his mistakes became part of their routine and they became a comedy folk singing duo and got a tv show and made a lot of money..." "What's unique about you?" he added. "Use that." Then he asked me, "How are your grades?"

"As, Bs, Cs..." I said.

"Good," he said. "Some people with dyslexia, they can't function in school at all."

He went on, "When I was in high school, my guidance counselor, Mr. Neal, called my mother in. I was sitting right there when he said, 'Ms. Leno, have you thought of taking Jay out of school?' He said, 'education is not for everyone.' And I said, 'hey, I'm in the room!' And he said, 'McDonalds has a training program.'

"I didn't want to work at McDonalds..." Jay chuckled. "By the way, we're still friends. In fact, I invited him on The Tonight Show. I introduced him as the guy who told me I should work at McDonalds."

We both laughed.

Jay continued, "My mother always told me 'You're going to have to work twice as hard to get the same things as other kids.' Well, that's not fair, I thought, but I don't mind working twice as hard if I get the same things. And that's actually worked out for me."

He went on, "When I was first starting out, other guys would go out to the comedy club maybe once or twice a week and go out with girls other nights and I would go every night. So by the end of the month, I had five times as much stage time as they did. With dyslexia, if you have one thing you like, you focus on it like a laser and that will carry you."

He added, "You're a real go-getter, Aidan. I would guess you're the only kid in your school who has written a book?"

"Yeah," I said. Then I asked him, "Did you ever worry that things might not work out?"

"Sure," he said. "Every single day. I was in my mid-twenties and my friends were getting their first homes and I was working for $10 here or $20 there. I would sleep in the alley between 44th and Ninth. I couldn't afford a hotel in New York, so I would sleep behind the

trashcans. That was a terrible area. Prostitutes and...
I won't even tell you the other things. But this was the
life I chose so I just stuck with it."

"Wow," I mumbled to myself.

Do you have an agent?" he asked.

"My mom does," I said.

"Have they sent your book out?" he asked.

"Harper Collins just passed on it," I told him.

"I wouldn't get discouraged," Jay said, kindly. "They
turn down 99% of the books they read."

He paused, then said, "When I was on The Tonight
Show, the TV network would say, 'Jay, the show's good,
but we think you can do better.' Better? I'd think. Really?
They were always looking for something more. Then they
realized I was close and close worked for them."

We talked for a bit longer, then I said, "Listen,
I know you're busy..."

He said. "Aidan, I think you're doing real good. Don't
get discouraged."

"Thanks," I said, then added, "Really."

"Listen," he said, "let me give you my office number.
Call me if you want to talk again."

And we said goodbye.

Before he hung up, he said, "Aidan?"

"Yeah?" I said.

"So you didn't find a publisher right away..." his
voice trailed off.

"Yeah..." I said.

"Well, welcome to the real world."

And then he hung up.

We hung up.

Neither Mom nor I spoke for a moment. Then she
let out a long breath. She stood up and stretched. She
walked out and closed the door softly behind her. I lay
back on my carpet and stared up at the ceiling.

This is what I had wanted, right?

Yeah.

Well, why?

I don't know. I guess I thought that if someone like Jay Leno saw me as someone worth responding to then maybe I'd start seeing myself that way.

My eyes followed a crack across the ceiling that disappeared behind the bookshelf.

Had it worked? Had I changed?

No. Not really.

I was still Aidan Colvin, 10th grader at Early College STEM, with some good grades and some bad ones. I still had braces, big feet, no girlfriend... I hadn't grown any.

At least in height.

Had I grown in other ways?

Maybe.

I now understood that there wasn't any magic to becoming a great surgeon or sculptor, businessman or writer... filmmaker, inventor, economist, arctic explorer or even comedian. Dyslexic or not, you simply had to put in the time. Stay positive. And focused. Persist even when, or maybe especially when, in doubt.

And everyone has moments of doubt.

Even Jay Leno.

Did you get that? Even Jay Leno.

Is that what I needed to learn?

I watched my ceiling fan tiredly circle. My eyes found a wasp climbing up my wall. I let out a long breath and watched it reach the ceiling and then start to fly.

No. Not only that.

I shook my head.

The wasp crossed my room and hit the window. It fell onto the ledge and then began to climb the glass. I looked back up at the fan.

I think what I needed to learn is that this learning

difference that I've been trying so desperately to hide or compensate for for almost ten years turned out to be the very thing that led me to do this amazing project.

And look what happened.

Look what *can* happen when we realize that the very things we think are holding us back instead turn out to be the key to worlds we could never have imagined.

Just look what can happen.

ABOUT THE AUTHORS

Aidan Colvin prefers button downs to muscle-tees, *White Collar* over *The Walking Dead*, driving a Mini Cooper over his mother's minivan, and the color blue. He likes dogs more than cats, Sourpatch kids over Reece's peanut butter cups, rowing over running, and thinks short people get a bad wrap. After you put down this book, he encourages you to listen to the song "Somewhere Over the Rainbow," because you know what? Through this project, he's found that dreams do come true.

Liisa Ogburn, AKA "Mom," prefers summer to winter, a night in to a night out, a game of Hearts over *Call of Duty*, and the color tangerine. She has a wicked sweet tooth, takes pictures at inopportune moments, often says "What's the worst thing that could happen?" right before something bad does happen, and sometimes breaks into yodeling during her daughters' carpool. Through this project, she learned that sometimes the best thing you can do is shoot for the moon. Why not? You might land a lot closer than you can ever imagine.

COLOPHON

This book uses the typeface Dyslexie designed by Christian Boer, who has dyslexia himself and designed this font to improve his reading life. People with dyslexia often swap, rotate and flip letters without noticing. The problem is that some letters are too similar to each other. Dyslexie font is designed so that every letter is unique in its own form. This counters the rotation, flipping and reversal of the letters. In addition, the font has extra distance between the letters and between the words. Dyslexic people may also overlook the beginning of a sentence and read two sentences as one. Therefore, the capital letters are bolder so the reader will easily identify the beginning of a new sentence. This font is available for home use for free and can be downloaded at www.dyslexiefont.com

Made in the USA
Lexington, KY
05 February 2019